The Evolving Nature of Cybercrime: New Trends Affecting Women in the Digital Space

Author:

Dr. Harshita Thalwal

TABLE OF CONTENTS

TITLE	PAGE NO.

DECLARATION BY THE CANDIDATE	ii
CERTIFICATE	iii
CERTIFICATE	iv
CERTIFICATE	v
ACKNOWLEGDEMENT	vi
CONTENTS TABULATION	vii - x
ABBREVATIONS	xi
CASE LAWS TABULATION	xii
1. CHAPTER 1: INTRODUCTION	1
1.1 CONCEPT OF CYBER CRIME	2
1.2 DEFINITION	3

1.3.1 CLASSIFICATION OF CYBER CRIME
    1.3.2 TRADITIONAL CYBERCRIME
    1.3.3 GENERAL CYBERCRIME
	3-5

1.4 TYPES OF CYBERCRIMES	5-10
1.5 REASONS FOR INCREASE IN CYBERCRIME	11-13
1.6 VICTIMIZATION OF WOMEN IN CYBER WORLD	13-14
1.7 CLASSIFICATION OF CYBERCRIMES AGAINST WOMEN	14-19
1.8 RESEARCH REPORT: A SCRUTINIZED STUDY OF CYBERCRIME AGAINST WOMEN IN INDIA	20-23
1.9 IMPACT OF CYBERCRIME ON WOMEN AND SOCIETY	23-29
1.10 EVOLUTION OF CYBERCRIME '	29-31
1.11 LEGAL FRAMEQORK SAFEGUARDING INTEREST OF WOMEN IN CYBER SPACE	32-33
1.12 LITERATURE REVIEW	34-42
1.13 PROBLEM PROFILE	43

1.14 RESEARCH QUESTION	44
1.15 RESEARCH METHODOLGY	44
1.16 OBJECTIVE OF STUDY	44-45
1.17 TENTATIVE CHAPTERISATION	45-46
2. CHAPTER II -EVOLUTION OF CYBER CRIME	
2.1 BACKGROUND	47
2.2 EMERGENCE OF INTERNET 2.2.1 HISTORICAL ACCOUNT OF INTERNET 2.2.2 CHANGING PATTERN OF INTERNET IN PRESENT TIME	48-54
2.3 PROS AND CONS OF INTERNET	54-59
2.4 CYBERCRIME: A HISTORICAL ACCOUNT	59-65
2.5 UBIQUITY OF CYBERCRIME	65-69
2.6 INTERNET AS A TOOL FOR CYBERWARFARE	70-71
2.7 CHRONOLGY OF REGULATIONS RELATING TO CYBER CRIME	71-75
2.8 CYBERCRIME IN CONTEMPORARY TIME	76-77
3. CHAPTER III- LEGAL PROVISIONS ON CYBERCRIME AGAINST WOMEN	
3.1 CYBERCRIME AND LAW	78
3.2 IMPORTANCE OF CYBER LAW	79-81
3.3 RELEVANT LAWS SAFEGUARDING THE INTEREST OF WOMEN AGAINST CYBERCRIME	81-82
3.4 CONSTITUTIONAL PROVISIONS SAFEGUARDING INTERESR OF WOMEN	83-93

3.5 RELEVANT PROVISIONS OF INDIAN CRIMINAL JUSTICE SYSTEM DEALING WITH RIGHTS OF WOMEN AGAINST CYBERCRIME	94

3.5.1 PROVISIONS UNDER IPC SAFEGUARDING WOMEN RIGHTS	95-102
3.6 CRIMINAL AMENDEMNET ACT, 2013	102-103
3.7 STATUTES DEALING WITH PROTECTION OF WOMEN IN VIRTUAL SPACE	103-114
3.8 LIABILITY OF INTERMEDIATOR	114-119
3.9 ROLE OF GOVERNMENT IN PROTECTING RIGHTS OF INDIVIDUAL IN CYBERSPACE	119
3.9.1 STEPS TAKEN BY GOVERNMENT OF INDIA TO CURB MENACE OF CYBERCRIME	120-123
3.10 A WAY FORWARD	123-124
3.11 LACUANE IN PRESENT LEGAL SYSTEM DEALING WITH MENACE OF CYBERCRIME AGAINST WOMEN	124-126
4. CHAPTER IV- ROLE OF JUDICIARY IN COMBATING CRIME AGAINST WOMEN IN CYBERSPACE	127-136
4.2 CHALLENGES FACED BY JUDICIARY IN CYBERSPACE	137-140
5. CHAPTER V – CYBERCRIME AGAINST WOMEN: A QUANTATIVE PICTURE	141-145
6 CHAPTER 6- CONCLUSION	
6.1 CONCLUSION	146-150
6.2 SUGGESTIONS	151-155

6 BIBLIOGRAPHY	
7.1 BOOKS	158
7.2 STATUTES	158

7.3 ARTICLES	159
7.4 NEWSPAPER	159
7.5 WIBLIOGRAPHY	160

ABBREVIATIONS

A.I.R	ALL INDIA REPORT
CS	CYBER SPACE
Cr.P.C	CODE OF CRIMINAL PROCEDURE
HC	HIGH COURT
ITC	INFORMATION TECHNOLOGY COMMUNICATION

IT	INFORMATION TECHNOLOGY
I.P.C	INDIAN PENAL CODE
I.S.P	INTERNET SERVICE PROVIDER
LGBTQ	LESBIAN, GAYS, BISEXUAL AND TRANSGENDER
NCW	NATIONAL COMMISSION FOR WOMEN
POCSO	PROTECTION OF CHILDREN FROM SEXUAL OFFENCES
SC	SUPREME COURT
SCC	SUPREME COURT CASES
VAW	VIOLENCE AGAINST WOMEN
WWW	WORLD WIDE WEB

TABLE OF CASE LAWS

Avinash Bajaj vs. State of Delhi	A.I.R 2008
Balan vs. State of Kerala	A.I.R 2003, 436
Dr. L Prakash vs. State of Tamil Nadu	A.I.R 2002
K. Puttaswamy vs. Union of India	A.I.R (2017) 10 SCC 1
Ritu Kohli vs. Manish Kathuria	A.I.R 2001
Saddam Hussain vs. State of M.P	(2016) SCC 1411

Santosh Kumar vs. Union of India (Through CBI)	2007 CriLJ 964, 133(2006) DLT 393
Shreya Singhal vs. Union of India	A.I.R 2015 SCC 1523
Suhas Katti vs. State of Tamil Nadu	A.I.R 2004, 4680
State of West Bengal vs. Animesh Boxi	A.I.R 2017, 1587

CYBER CRIME AGAINST WOMEN: A BRIEF ANALYSES

CHAPTER 1

1.INTRODUCTION

World presently has become a global village by the virtue of Internet space, which is in both ways a blessing and a curse depending upon the intent behind its usage. Post the advent of industrial revolution during late eighteenth to early nineteenth century, the human civilization holistically in various material dimensions has evolved at a rapid pace; so much so that, in the last few decades technology has become an inseparable part and parcel of our lifestyle. It has brought about a radical change not only in our traditional ways to connect with people or aspects of lifestyle but has even modernized our society too in a revolutionizing way. But technological progress cannot be seen as an implication of progress in terms of creating value driven society. With internet nowadays covering myriad aspects of our lives, it in many ways makes us dependent and more susceptible towards the wrongdoings and malpractices that happens over the internet by hackers aimed towards the exploitation of users in many forms, viz, account hacking, blackmailing, frauds, etc.

INTERNET with its invention in this century is seen as an era from where technological advancement is demarcated as pre and post internet age. Looking back at the time when it was invented no would have ever thought that one day it will become an important facet of our daily requirements. Internet has become a platform of communication, where people have easy access to communicate with others irrespective of geographical barriers. It serves as a huge platform where not only one can communicate with their loved ones who lives overseas but even provides any sort of information just at a click. There are around 4.66 billion active user of internet users worldwide, which forms 60% of the world population and among them 92% of them has direct access to internet service through their mobile phones.[1] The aforementioned figures clearly states that half of the world population is having direct access to internet connectivity. Internet has totally changed our lifestyle as everything is available in online mode and you are just a click away from getting any information, to do window shopping, or carry out any business transactions and even online studies has become a trend. Nowadays, we are totally dependent on internet services even to carry out any minimal work

---

[1] Internet Users in The World, available at: *https://www.statistic.com* (last visited on May 25, 2021)

and this overdependence on internet has paved a room for criminal acts namely CYBER CRIME.

There is no doubt that internet has made our life better but it even made a room for the notorious elements in our society to carry out criminal activities against the internet users. On one hand Internet served as a boon for mankind by easing out his day-to-day activity and making life better but on the other hand it acted as a bane for human civilization due to the victimization of an individual in the cyber world. On an average, every third internet user has once in a life fallen prey to some kind of cyber offence. Cybercrime continues to rise on a larger scale by becoming more complex and fragile in nature, thus, affecting the essential services, businesses and private individuals' life alike. It has become a globally recognized crime which has a great impact on every individual and society as a whole. The surge in cybercrime cases is a matter of concern and there is a need to formulate effective policies to put a check on any criminal act and avoid victimization of any person at instance of cybercriminals.

1.1 CONCEPT OF CYBER CRIME

Cybercrime is becoming a global plague - new technologies provide anonymity to criminals and an increasing number of people lured by a chance of becoming rich in a quick and easy way are getting engaged in this type of criminal activity. Cybercrime is one of the fastest and ever-growing form of crime in present time. Due to the rampant globalization of internet service and its easy accessibility to all gave an opportunity to criminals to exploit the internet users for their personal interest. The concept of cybercrime is not an old phenomenon, rather it was after the invent of internet and digitalization that the cases of cyber-crimes came into limelight. Earlier the information and communication technologies were used to carry out political, economic and social work only, but in recent times every individual has direct access to its usage and this has escalated the speed of cybercrimes. Further, the crimes committed in online mode are very peculiar in nature and it becomes difficult to understand the pattern of criminal intent and identify the real offenders due to the anonymity of such users. These crimes are committed in cyberspace which is a virtual world with no borders, thus, enabling the criminals to carry out a wide range of illegal- computer related activities such as identity theft, industrial espionage, defamation, data breach, dissemination of offensive sexual material in cyber-space, money laundering in electronic form, tax evasion, cyber-terrorism, fraud, etc.[2]

1.2 DEFINITION

In a general sense cybercrime is said to be computer related offences which are committed behind the curtains in virtual world.

Cybercrime is defined as a crime which involves computer devices to target the victim in digital mode or a crime in which usually a computer system is used to carry out criminal offences.[3]

Cybercrime is also called computer crimes, where computer devices are used as an instrument to further illegal ends, such as committing fraud, trafficking in child pornography, identity theft, or violating privacy. These crimes are generally committed through the medium of internet, as its importance has grown in the field of entertainment, education, commerce and government work.[4]

Cybercrime is a criminal activity that targets the computer devices or a network device, whereby the criminals use these devices to carry out offences against the government, corporate sector or any individual user.

Cybercrime can be elaborated as an act of criminal nature committed via digital modes through different means of communication to attain certain pecuniary gain. It covers a wide range of criminal activities such as fraud, money laundering, drug trafficking, identity theft, copyright related offence etc.

Cybercrime is a criminal offence which is committed on the Web, it is a criminal offence regarding the Internet, a violation of laws on the Internet, an illegality committed with regard to the Internet, breach of law on the Internet, computer crime, contravention through the Web, corruption regarding Internet, disrupting operations through malevolent programs on the Internet, electric crime, sale of contraband on the Internet, stalking victims on the Internet and theft of identity on the Internet."[5]

According to Organization for Economic Cooperation and Development (OCED) "The computer related crimes can be defined as any illegal, unethical or unauthorized behavior that involves automatic processing or transmission of data".[6]

---

[2] Prof. N.V. Paranjape, *Criminology, Penology, Victimology* 167 (Central Law Publication, Allahabad, 17th edn., 2018)
[3] Definition Of Cybercrime, *available at:* https://www.merriam-webster.com (last visited on May 25, 2021)
[4] Cybercrime, available at: https://www.wikipedia.in (last visited on May 25, 2021)
[5] Cybercrime and Privacy, The Centre for Internet and Society, *available at:* https://cis-india.org (last visited on May 25, 2021)

1.3 CLASSIFICATION OF CYBER CRIME

Looking at the nature of cybercrime, it is broadly divided into 2 main spectrum and these are:

1. THE TRADITIONAL CLASSIFICATION
2. THE GENERAL CLASSIFICATION

1.3.1 TRADITIONAL CLASSIFICATION:

The idea of classifying cybercrime into traditional category is suggested by *SIBER*, and it includes mainly two distinct types of cybercrimes, namely (1) Cybercrime related to economic aspects and (2) Cybercrimes against privacy.[7]The primary aim behind any criminal act being carried out in virtual world in the form of cybercrime is usually done for profit making. The economic type of cybercrimes include fraud committed through malware, illegal copying of software of the targeted person, password cracking, computer spying, computer sabotage, counterfeiting of currency through electronic medium, electronic money laundering, theft of personal data, etc. All of these economic crimes are carried through computer devices by hacking the system of an individual or any corporate firm and getting all relevant information from their accounts. The cybercrime in economic sphere is at rise. In a report submitted by The Centre for Strategic and International Studies (CSIS), it was found that on an average round about $600 billion, nearly one percent of Global GDP, is lost to the cybercrimes annually.[8]With the expansion of online business and online transactions, the economic crimes are also getting more enhanced than ever before. Among all the economic cybercrime the most common and prevalent offences are atm fraud, white collar crimes, drug trafficking and hacking the accounts of corporate firms or of any individual person.

On the other hand, cybercrime against individual privacy is quite different from economic cybercrime as it adversely affects the judicial right of privacy of a person. Cybercrime violates individuals' privacy and hinder with the security of their data, particularly password hacking, malware, identity theft, financial fraud, medical fraud, and certain grave offences against persons such as publishing defamatory content about the targeted person to tarnish the dignity of an individual. Cyber harassment, cyber bullying, child pornography, publishing

---

[6] *Ibid*
[7] *Ibid 2*
[8] Cybercrime: A Threat to Person, Property and Society, available at: https://papers.ssrn.com (last visited on May 25, 2021)

offensive material against the vulnerable group of society etc., are some of the most prevalent forms of offences which are being committed against an individual in the virtual world. The main reason behind a sudden rise in the number of instances of cyber-crimes against individual privacy is due to the coming up of social media sites. With the coming up of social media, the trend of posting everything on these communications' platform made it easier for the criminals to invade into personal sphere of the user and target them for their own interest.

1.3.2 GENERAL CLASSIFICATION

A more general interpretation of cybercrimes may be possibly be said to be as

(1) Cybercrime against all forms of property in general and

(2) Cybercrime committed against State or society.

Cybercrime against property is one of the most prominent offence which is carried in virtual world just to gain monetary profit out of it. Computer related offences which target the property encompasses computer vandalism, virus transmission, violation of intellectual property rights, copyright infringement, unauthorized access over computer, data breach, internet time theft, sale of illegal articles etc.[9] These crimes are usually committed against business firms, banks or any fiscal body which deals with finance related issues.

Cybercrime against state or society usually comprises of offence of cyber terrorism, possessing unauthorized information, counterfeiting of currency, disseminating fake information among the masses, online gambling, money laundering in electronic form, forgery, distributing pirated software, posting explicit content on internet, child pornography, etc. Cyber terrorism is one distinct kind of crime which is being committed by an individual or group in order to threaten the international governments and the citizens, with the aim of shaking the foundation of any government. The Parliament Attack in Delhi is one such example of cybercrime against state which shook the whole nation integrity.[10] While cybercrime against society includes such offences, which target the vulnerable section of society and comprises of crimes such as: child pornography, outraging the modesty of women by publishing obscene content about her in cyberspace, human trafficking, extortion. These criminal acts adversely affect the moral sanctity of our society to a great extent.

1.4 TYPES OF CYBERCRIMES

---

[9] *Supra 2 170*
[10] *Ibid 8*

Cybercrimes are generally referred as computer related offences which are carried out in the virtual world whose dimension is vast and is borderless. The common types of computer related offences are as follow:

1.4.1 HACKING: Hacking is one of the most common form of cybercrime these days. Hacking process has been a part of computing for 40 years. The prominent reason behind hacking any system vary from person to person, as some may indulge in act of hacking for the sake of enjoyment and thrill while for some do it for monetary gains or out of political interest. In simple terms hacking can be defined as an unauthorized access of someone personal data through computer network.[11] There have been reported instances where the passwords or accounts of the internet users are hacked and their personal data is stolen either for fun or to precure some monetary benefit out of it by blackmailing the targeted person. According to a study it was found that every 39 second instances of hacking take place around the globe.[12] Hacking may be carried out in various forms such as:

- **WEBSITE HACKING**: It is a specie of hacking where the hacker through unauthorized means hacks the website of the victim and gather all relevant information about the victim and use the same against him.

- **E-MAIL HACKING:** E-mail is a new method of communication which is widely used nowadays. This platform of communication is mostly used to send and receive formal information which consist of personal and confidential information of an individual. If an email account is hacked it gives an easy access to the hackers to read the messages which are sent or received by the legitimate owner. Thus, the hacker might use the sensitive information of the victim either to get monetary benefit or to exploit the image of such person.[13]

- **PASSWORD HACKING:** Password hacking is a method of recovering password from the computer devices through the data transmitted or files stored in computers. In simple terms it can be defined as a process to obtain authorized password to get an easy access to an account or device by use of unauthorized means and methods.

CYBER TERRORISM:

---
[11] *Supra 2 172*
[12] Website Hacking Statistics, *available at: https://patchstack.com* (last visited on May 25, 2021)
[13] Email hacking, *available at: https://en.m.wikipedia.in* (last visited on May 25, 2021)

Every nation state and international bodies are working together in the direction of curbing the menace of terrorism, which has rippling effect on the people, politics and economic state around the world. World has witnessed the brutality faced by the victims of terrorist attacks. The terrorist groups always find new ways to engage into terrorist activities in order to create threat in the mind of citizens and spread violence all around the world. Despite having all sort of border security, terrorism has been a very complex issue for any government. Furthermore, with the emergence of new communication technologies and internet facilities, the mode of terrorism has undergone a dramatic change by enhancing its mode of operation through virtual world, thus, giving birth to new terrorism activity known as "CYBER TERRORISM".

"Cyber terrorism can be defined as a deliberated act which is politically motivated with the intention to attack the computer system, get unauthorized access to confidential information and data, which ultimately results in violence against citizens targeted by sub national or secret agents".[14] Cyber terrorism has domestic and international complications. The most sensitive area which is prone to be attacked by the cyber terrorist are military installations of nation, power plants, banks, government departments, air traffic control, telecommunication services, etc. Cyber terrorism has become one of the modern ways of spreading terrorism around the globe due to the easy access of internet facilities. Moreover, cyberspace provides a safe room for the terrorist to hide their identity to carry out attack under the veil of anonymity and evade prosecution. With the inter- connectivity of national networks, it becomes relatively easy for the terrorist groups to directly affect a large section of society at the same time. Therefore, it is the need of the hour to develop new security policies for combating cyber terrorism.

MONEY LAUNDERING:

The internet service brings convenience in carrying out daily activities with an ease and money laundering is no exception to it. In virtual world the other name given to money laundering is known as Cyber Laundering. Among all the financial crimes facilitated by internet, money laundering through online means has drawn significant attention due to its gigantic size and the various methods used by the perpetrators to

---

[14] Dr. Jaswinder Singh, Legal Essays & Articles for Competitions (Chawla Publications Ltd, Chandigarh)

legitimize ill-gotten profit and evade prosecution. The term cyber-laundering can be simply defined as malpractice of carrying out money laundering in the cyberspace by way of online transactions. In its principle, cyber-laundering shares same feature as that to conventional money laundering where money is obscured by illegal means and is placed into a legal financial system to evade prosecution.

Unlike the traditional or conventional money laundering, the cyber laundering provides a better opportunity to the perpetrators by offering them a wide range of options which are less costly, speedier and easy to carry money laundering through online transactions. With the help of internet facilities, the act of cyber laundering can be carried out easily from any corner of the world without any fear of being caught. The online-service providers such as banks and are more prone to fall prey to money launderers as they provide wide range of financial services to its users. With the passage of time online -gambling has gained a momentum as the safest web- based platform where the money of tax evasion is legitimized smoothly. As the online-gambling can be carried out from any part of the world, it becomes quite difficult to investigate such cases and due to anonymity in the cyber world it's difficult to find real offender, thus, giving an easy hand to offender to carry out financial crimes with an ease.[15] Internet protects the offender where they can hide their identity and carry criminal activities from any part of world and this has contributed towards economic offences which hampers the overall development of nation. Electronic money laundering and tax evasion create a gap between rich and poor which results into increase in other offences which are committed against human body and property to fulfill basic needs.

ONLINE FRAUD:

Fraud is defined as misrepresentation of facts and information, whereby the offender withholds the important information or states false information to the victim in order to gather relevant information from him and gain monetary benefit out of it. When an act of fraud is committed in virtual world through online medium it is called as Online Fraud. Online fraud usually involves financial fraud and identity theft. Online fraud can be committed by virus attack on computer system or any other devices to retrieve

---

[15] Cyber laundering: An Analyses of Typology and Techniques, *available at: https://search.proquest.com* (last visited on May 26, 2021)

the personal data of the victim. Phishing and spamming are the two most common form of online fraud that takes place in virtual world.[16]

DATA DIDDLING:

Data Diddling is one of the cybercrimes in which the original data is altered in the database by means of virus attack or malware functioning. It is usually conducted by having unauthorized access to the computer system and is generally resorted for the purpose of illegal monetary benefit or for committing financial scam.

CYBER DEFAMATION:

Defamation means causing an injury to the reputation of a person by publishing a statement against him which tends to lower down the dignity of a person in the eyes of right-minded people in society.[17] A defamatory statement is one which exposes the victim of such act to humiliation and disgrace in the society. Such statement may be made in oral form or in written form with an intention on the part of offender to impede the reputation of victim by portraying wrong image of such person in the mind of like-minded people in society. When such disreputable statements are published in the virtual world by online mode with an intention to cause injury to the user reputation, is known as Cyber Defamation. Cyber Defamation is caused in cyber space against any person in order to bring disgrace to his reputation through various means of electronic devices. It engulfs in its ambit an individual or any company or any institution in order to bring disrepute to his name and fame.

Cyber Defamation is same in nature as defamation in torts but the only difference between them is that defamation is committed in real world whereas cyber defamation is committed in cyber space. But the magnitude of intention is the same that is to tarnish the reputation of victim.

IDENTITY THEFT:

Identity theft is a crime of obtaining any personal or confidential or financial information of an individual by unauthorized means in order to use such information to carry out illegal activities such as fraud, personation, blackmailing, or injuring the

---

[16] Online Frauds-Classification and Cases, available at: *https://indiaforensic.com* (last visited on May 26, 2021)
[17] Dr. R.K Bangia, *Law of Torts* 146, (Allahabad Law Regency, Haryana, 23rd edn. 2015)

reputation of the innocent person. The incidence of identity theft is increasing day by day with the coming up of online transactions and advanced computer technologies. The identity thieves use new technologies to gather the confidential information to commit identity fraud. They may hack the computer system of an individual or browse the social networking sites or use deceptive mails or messages to get all personal information about the targeted victim.[18]

VIRUS DISSEMINATION:

In scientific terms viruses are defined as a computer programs that infect a system or files present in the system, and have a tendency to be circulated to other computers or other networking devices. The effect of virus is that it disrupts or destroy the computer operation and affect the data which is stored in computers – either by bringing changes in them or by deleting it altogether at once. Computer virus is malicious code that is represented by copying itself to another program, and usually spread via removeable media or through internet. A computer virus spreads between systems after some type of human intervention. In other words, viruses require someone to knowingly or unknowingly spread the infection between system. Once a virus enters in any infected system, it remains there for a longer period of time. [19]

INTELLECTUAL PROPERTY CRIMES:

Intellectual property rights refer to a bundle of rights which protects the original work or idea of the creator that consist of: domain name, any literary work, design, symbol or logo which is used in commerce. All these ideas and work are new creation and is given the status of personal rights and is protected under Intellectual Property Law. But with the modernization of technology and easy access to internet there have been many instances where these rights are violated by the perpetrator by committing piracy, copyright infringement, trade-mark violations, theft of computer code etc. Digitalization facilitated the perpetrators to have unauthorized access to the new ideas and designs and provided them a platform where they can easily copy these ideas and sell them illegally. Computer piracy is one of the examples of violation of intellectual rights where, the hacker generally steals away the valuable intellectual property content by copying it and sell it to the user at low rate. Thus, copying of any material

---
[18] Identity Theft Definition, *available at: https://www.investopedia .com* (last visited on May 26, 2021)
[19] The 12 Types of Cybercrime, *available at: https: www.digit.in* (last visited on May 26, 2021)

and selling it in pirated form is against copyright and the offender is punished in pursuance of law.[20]

Trademark is also one of the kinds of Intellectual Property rights that usually protects the good-will and reputation of the traders. These marks are used to differentiate among the various goods of a traders from those of other traders who work in same stream of business. But unfortunately, with digitalization of the commercial market, the hackers usually copy the original trade mark of the trader in order to sell inferior goods in the name of traders and cause injury to his reputation. With the coming up of online shopping, the instances of inferior products being sold out in the name of trader is common nowadays. The liability of offender does arise, but sometimes it becomes difficult to track the master mind behind the violation of these proprietary rights due to anonymity and borderless dimension of cyber space.

1.5 REASONS FOR INCREASE IN CYBER CRIMES:

In this modern era, we are living in a world of digital technology where everything is influenced by the internet connectivity services. Whether it's about storing data or getting easy access to the information, we seek assistance from the internet to get our work done. Every internet user spends most of his time on social media or any other entertainment platform and even carry out his daily work in online mode. Thereby, this ever-growing involvement of users in the cyber world makes them prone to cyber threats. There's no room for doubt that instances of cyber-crimes are increasing at a mounting pace. The perpetrators or hackers exploit the internet users by intruding into their personal information through unauthorized access for their own entertainment or interest. The number of cyber-attacks in the virtual world tends to grow faster with the passage of time. With the rapid development of new innovative technologies and cyber mechanisms, the internet criminals are using the world wide web as a platform to attack the internet users and are becoming more powerful than ever. They are continuously using new technologies to hack the internet world to get the confidential information of the users, so that it could be used against the users to victimize them and get monetary benefit out of it. The foremost reason behind increase in cyber offences are as follow:

- **EASY ACCESS TO INTERNET SERVICES:**

---

[20] *Supra 2 175*

Today almost half of the world population has a direct access to internet services either through computers or mobile phone. Due to the easy accessibility of internet services, and technological advancement it has become easy for the offender to get unauthorized access to the computer system of another person or hack their mobile device and social media accounts to gather all relevant information about such person and use the same to commit cybercrime against the innocent party.

- **ANONYMITY IN VIRTUAL WORLD:**

Anonymity in general sense is defined as a situation where the name or place of person is not known. The anonymity on internet is relatable to the aforementioned definition. Internet anonymity is quite prevalent where the user hides his real identity while communicating with other fellow users. The anonymity in the cyber space might be important to hide your personal information from others to whom the users don't wish to communicate. But the same is even used by the cyber criminals to carry cyber offences. The cyber criminals usually the hackers use the internet anonymity as a way to carry out crimes such as drug trafficking, electronic money laundering, fraud, theft, human trafficking etc. in cyber space. Due to anonymity of the criminal in cyber space it becomes difficult for the law agencies to trace the actual offender and punish him. It is only in rare cases that the cyber criminals are caught red handed while committing cyber offences. This is the main reason for increase in cybercrimes at present.

- **LACK OF AWARENESS:**

Another common factor which leads to cyber offences is lack of awareness. Most of the internet users lack adequate knowledge about the cyber-attacks. Many instances of atm and credit card fraud have been reported by the victim and the main reason behind this is that people are unbale to understand the pattern of criminal intent of the fraud messages or calls. Internet might be easily accessible to all, but only few are aware of malware attacks that could breach the privacy of the user to gather all information about them and they become victim of cyber offences.

- **ADDICTION:**

The saying "Excess of Everything is Dangerous" religiously apply to internet addiction. Today, the most common health issue among the youth is mental health disorder. The main cause behind the deteriorating mental health condition of young people is due to the excessive use of mobile devices and internet. The rapid growth in the Information Technology especially with coming up of internet services and social media sites have made people more less like robots who spend most of their time surfing net.

On an average every third internet user is addict to it, and suffers from internet addiction. This over dependence of every individual on internet makes it easy for the criminals to victimize the targeted person. People spend most of their time on social media interacting with people in cyber space rather then in real world, and this leads to emotional stress and people suffer from anxiety disorder and some might end up going into state of depression. While the cyber criminals always look for such internet user who is more emotionally unstable and are considered as soft target for them. Women and youth are the most prominent victim of the cybercrime. They can be easily influenced and victimized in cyber space.

- **LACK OF EFFICIENT LEGISLATIONS**:

Law has a significant role to play in every society in order to maintain peace and order and eliminate crime from society. We have laws to regulate misconduct of individual in our society to avoid any malpractice occurring from such act. While internet related crimes or cyber crime are becoming graver and more intense in nature. Today most of the traditional crimes are carried out through online, leading to increase in crime rate. It becomes quite difficult to regulate the criminal activities online due to inefficient legal statues. Thus, giving an opportunity to habitual offender to carry all malpractices online without any fear of punishment. Therefore, it is the need of the hour to have efficient machinery to regulate online platform and penalize the culprit for violating the rights of victim.

1.6 VICTIMIZATION OF WOMEN IN CYBER WORLD

Looking at the present scenario, it can be asserted that violence against women is rising at an alarming rate. Violence against women (VAW) which is peculiarly known as gender-based violence and sexual and gender-based violence (SGBV) are considered those acts which are violent in nature and exclusively committed against women or girls. These offences are gender- based and the offender usually target the vulnerable section of society especially women and girls in any forms. The VAW has a vast history, it is as old as the society itself and the intensity of such violence vary from time to time between societies.[21] Since ancient period, women have always been subjected to all sorts of violence in comparison to the male section of society. The reason behind such violence in literal sense generally arises from the sense of entitlement, male predominance in the society, superiority complex, or the socio-cultural aspect of patriarchal setup.

The notion that "women is slave to men and not an equal of men" is still practiced in our society today and they are subjected to violence and cruelty. Violence against women can fit into several broad categories and it includes sexual offences as rape, sexual harassment, domestic violence, acid attacks, reproductive coercion, female infanticide, prenatal sex selection, obstetric violence, as well as there are some customary or traditional practices such as honor killings, dowry violence, female genital mutilation and forced marriage by abduction. Other than these grave offences the perpetrators commit against women at a larger scale which includes: trafficking in women and forced prostitution by organized criminal network groups.[22]

With the coming up of internet facilities and online communication apps, the crimes against women have totally evolved from traditional violence to virtual violence. Even in the virtual committed in cyberspace. The crimes committed against women might differ in nature than the traditional crimes, but the reason for gender-based victimization remains the same. Cybercrimes against women are on raise and they are drastically victimized in cyber world. The most prevalent cybercrimes against women are: cyber defamation, sexual offences, pornography, online grooming fraud, blackmailing, trafficking in women and girls, stalking, breach of privacy etc. This evolution of criminal act committed against womanhood has raised many apprehensions regarding the cyber security and the laws regulating the same.

1.7 CLASSIFICATION OF CYBERCRIMES AGAINST WOMEN:

The rapid growth in the area of Information and Communication Technology (ICT) has significantly brought a drastic change in our day-to-day social life. It has bridged the gap of communication that existed prior to the coming up of internet services. There is no doubt that the internet has made our lifestyle easy and comfortable, but unfortunately our over dependence on it has opened its door for the criminal activities as well. Among all the ICT users, the male counterpart is more prone to face the brunt of the online offences that takes

---

[21] Violence Against Women, *available at:* https://enwikipedia.org (last visited on May 28, 2021)
[22] *Ibid*

place every minute in cyber space. The most prominent types of cybercrimes committed against women and young girls are:

CYBER STALKING:

Cyberstalking is one of the cybercrimes committed against women. Cyber stalking is generally committed by stalking or harassing women over internet forum. In a literal sense it means targeting any individual or organization to defame such person or create threat in the mind of victim. Cyber stalking may take place in various forms, but relatively in broader sense it takes place via online mode. The growing trend of being active on social media sites such as Facebook, WhatsApp, Twitter, Snapchat etc., gives an opportunity to the perpetrators to gather all personal information about the user and use the same to exploit or harass the user. The women user of these social media sites is more vulnerable to and easy target to exploit. The perpetrators keep a check on the daily activity on the account of the targeted women or girl and this paves a way to stalking. These cyber stalkers collect all the personal data of a woman and uses the same to terrorize her by sending displeasing messages or images in a row several times a day.[23]

Nowadays cyberstalking is becoming a menace for women in virtual world. The nature of cyber stalking might change its nature from a simple act to grave one and can further develop into physical abuse of the victim. As longer as the instance of cyber stalking goes on, it welcomes more and more problem for the women who get harassed and faces emotional and mental turmoil. The fact is that cyberstalking goes unnoticed because it doesn't involve any kind of physical contact between the perpetrator and the victimized women or girl but in the longer run it might change into real life stalking and abuse.

CYBER TROLLING AND GENDER BASED BULLYING:

Recently, with the expansion of internet services and with the birth of social media, the cybercrimes have taken a new shape and has extended its roots deep in our society. The two new modes of targeting the women in cyberspace are trolling and cyber bulling. Trolling and bullying are the vicious acts performed by the perpetrators to injure the reputation of the victim and even agitate hate crime against them.

---

[23] What Cyber Stalking Is and How to Prevent It, available at: https://www.tripwire.com (last visited on May 28, 2021)

Trolling on various topics have become a source of entertainment on social media platform. Trolling is recognized as deliberately inflicting hatred among various groups of society, racism, causing mental agony to the victim etc. Umpteenth number of platforms over internet provides free access to online trolling and having less or none at all regulations keeping a check over it and lack of punitive measures too makes internet space toxic to mental health and sometimes giving some platforms a disreputable name.

GENDER BASED BULLYING AND TARGETING OVER INTERNET SPACE-

Female section is the most exploited section when it comes to the real-world cases of cyber bullying and gender bias. They are subjected to such cybercrimes due to many reasons and most of them are at times sexually motivated. Scamsters targets such women who are imbecile and more prone to phishing frauds, and privacy related scams owing to lack of knowledge in terms of internet and online platforms. Such exploitations are more general than what media reports makes us believe as unreported cases exceeds the reported ones in this matter.

Not only females sometimes even the most aware netizens become target of many online frauds because of subtle and organized ways of scamsters and fraudsters in order to establish their objectives which are always on the darker side. Thus, it become imperative to have awareness and knowledge of the online world before making one's identity easily discoverable to hackers and using, rather, misusing the privacy related information. The old adage henceforth is most suited here i.e., prevention is always better than cure, and only prevention here is to become a cautious and intelligent netizen to prevent exploitation of any kind over the internet.

CYBER TROLLING - A CASE STUDY

One of the first high-profile cases emerged in the US state of Missouri in 2006, when 13-year-old Megan Meier took her own life after being bullied online. **Megan Taylor Meier** (November 6, 1992 – October 17, 2006) was an American teenager who was subjected to cyber bulling and as a result, she committed suicide as a consequence of bulling in cyber world.[24]

Let's take another case of Cathy Sierra or Anna Mayer, where these two girls were bullied in virtual world and later on it got graver and turned into hostile hatred crime. With the rapid

---

[24] Debarati Halder and K. Jaishankar, *Cybercrimes Against Women in India 43* (Sage Publication, Delhi, 2017)

growth of social networking sites, the nature of cyber bullying has drastically changed from a simple text message to publishing explicit images of the victim on websites.

Cyber bulling or trolling in the digital world is not just limited to women but even the trans women are more vulnerable to be bullied. Bulling in any form cannot be justified, as it has a great impact on the social life and mental status of the victim. The act of bullying usually turns out to be grave and dangerous for the victim survival. It has a socio-psychological impact on those who are bullied, as they may feel traumatised and suffer from withdrawal symptoms and in some case might commit suicide. Thus, it becomes an important issue to be considered by the law-making body to keep check on such activities and upheld the accountability of offender.

SEXUAL OFFENCES AGAINST WOMEN IN CYBER WORLD

Crime against women in society has been prevailing in our society since ages. Even today in this modern era women are more prone to become victim at the instance of offender. Crime against women has been prevailing in our society since ages. Even today in this modern era women are more prone to become victim at the instance of offender. The commission of crime against women can be committed in any form and at any place. The reason behind victimization of women may vary from society to society. Sexual violence is extremely negative and traumatic life incidence which effects the victim psychological and sociological affair to a great extent. It often gives rise to a wide range of socio-cultural brunt faced by the victim. It increases the sense of emotional helplessness and incompetency in the victim, thus, affecting their self-esteem and make them vulnerable to further violence.

With the advancement of the communication technology and easy access of internet services the threat of sexual violence against women in cyber space has emerged as a matter of concern. The growing trend of using various social media sites to communicate with people has paved a way for harassment of women in the virtual world. The perpetrators use new means and methods to commit gender-based cybercrime particularly against female, as they can be easily targeted, supressed and harassed for their own interest. The major type of sexual violence committed against women in virtual world are as: cyber pornography, cyber defamation, cyber harassment, blackmailing, identity theft, offences of online grooming etc. The offences of sexual violence traumatize the victim and they usually suffer from mental health problem such as withdrawal symptoms, anxiety disorder, depression etc. The social stigma resulting from sexual abuse is very prominent in the Asian cultures where anything related with sexual connotations is highly stigmatized as there is male dominance in the society and they hold prejudices to blame the victim for any wrongdoing omitted against them.

- **CYBER HARASSMENT**:

Violence against women (VAW) is quite common around the world. Women are more vulnerable to exploitation and sexual harassment even in the cyber space. Cyber harassment against women generally include-stalking, sending obscene content to particular women, bullying women based on her sexual orientation, blackmailing her, eve teasing etc. The subjugation and exploitation of women in the cyber space has an adverse effect on the personal and social life if the victim. Online harassment cases have increased many folds, posing a grave threat to the right of women in cyberspace. Victimization of women in the cyber space especially sexually harassing them for monetary benefit is getting more frequent than ever before. Thus, having a far-reaching impact on the mental state of victim.

- **CYBER DEFAMATION**

Defamation in a general sense means publishing such content about an individual in written or oral form which brings disrepute to him /her by causing injury to his dignity.[25] Cyber defamation is same as the conventional form of defamation, but the only difference that exist is that cyber defamation is committed by publishing any content without the knowledge of other person on internet by means of video, audio, or any image which causes injury to the reputation of the victim. Cyber defamation is one of the crimes to which women and young girls are often subjected by the offender for their personal interest. The offender might publish any image or transmit a fake information about women online to tarnish her image and bring disrepute to her in the society.

- **ONLINE GROOMING:**

This is a new form of cyber crime that is under rated and usually not reported. Online grooming is referred to a situation where two individuals communicate with each other focusing more on sexual conduct.[26] One of the most suitable examples of online grooming is the matrimonial sites. On these sites the groomer communicates with the women and forms a good relationship with them. In few cases it has been seen that the groom usually indulges in

---

[25] Dr. R.K Bangia, *Law of Torts* 149 (Allahabad Law Agency, Haryana 23rd edn. 2015)
[26] Online Grooming, available at: https://www.childline.org.uk (last visited on May 29, 2021)

sexual conversation with the women and use the same to blackmail her. Many instances have been reported where the groomer promise the women to marry and gather all necessary information about her and force her to indulge in sexual activities. There are many dating sites as well where dating fraud is quite common. On these sites people uploads their images and build online relationship with each other. The perpetrators usually look forward for such opportunity and select their soft targets by building an emotional relationship with victim and gain her trust with an intent to exploit her image in society. Cyber grooming has emerged as a big threat to women and young girls where the groomer sexually exploits the women and tend to escape the prosecution due to anonymity in the cyberspace. The main aim behind cyber grooming is to extort money from the victim through illegal means.

- **PRIVACY INFRINGEMENT:**

The right to privacy is a fundamental right to which an individual in entitled since his birth. Privacy is not only a matter of right but also a social obligation, no to interfere in someone personal space. But this moralistic approach doesn't seem to apply in the cyber space. Privacy infringement is a common phenomenon in the virtual world, where the perpetrator gathers all necessary information about the victim through all illegal means. Infringement of right to privacy may be considered as main problem in relation to crimes in cyber space based on gender discrimination. Data diddling and stealing the personal information about the victim is considered as privacy infringement. The reason for privacy infringement of women and young girls in the cyberspace might be as a result of seeking revenge, for sexual gratification or for gaining monetary benefits out of making adult -porn and sell it online. Additionally, by stealing the personal information about women the perpetrator uses it to represent a fake identity of such victim and use it for illegal means in order to malign the character of the victim and bring disregard to her from other fellow users.

TRAFFICKING OF WOMEN THROUGH VIRTUAL MODE:

Human trafficking is one of the most cruel and indecent crime that is committed against humanity. It is third most prominent crime that takes place around the world following drug trafficking and transportation of illegal weapons. Trafficking women and young girls is comparatively higher in number than men. The women and young girls are vulnerable to be trafficked and are forced to indulge in flesh trade, illegal sexual activities, drug trafficking and the old way of trafficking of women and young girls is taken over by internet platform. Today, women are being trafficked online, where they are sold and purchased by the buyer. Although trafficking of women for prostitution is an age-old crime but with the coming up of internet services and social media sites the menace of women trafficking and their exploitation is getting graver in nature day by day. As the world goes online, it becomes easy for the perpetrator to get in touch with the women from various parts of world and making it easy for them to commit crime against them. The perpetrator usually builds up relationship with the victim and promise to marry them or get them good job security at abroad. Women from destitute areas are poor and they get influenced by the proposal and become victim of trafficking. Women are considered as soft target in virtual world as they lack awareness about cyber offences and the suppression of women in our society provides opportunity for criminals to harass them in cyber space. The increasing trend of trafficking women and young girls through cyberspace has raised many apprehension over the security system of every nation, thus , emphasizing on the urgent of efficient machinery to curb the menace of cyber trafficking of women in virtual world.

1.8 RESEARCH REPORT: A SCRUTINIZED STUDY ON CRYBERCRIMES AGAINST WOMEN IN INDIA

1.8 BACKGROUND OF CYBERCRIMES AGAINST WOMEN IN INDIA: AN INFORMATIONAL ACCOUNT

As per National Crime Record Bureau Data Digital India may have become a soft target for criminals as country recorded a huge increase of 63.5 percent in cybercrime cases in the year 2019,

The NCRB's data further stated that 4,4546 cases of cybercrimes were registered in 2019 as compared to 28,248 in 2018.

The data showed in 60.4 percent of cases, registered fraud was the motive followed by sexual exploitation (5.1%) and causing disrepute (4.2%).

As per the data, in metropolitan cities, a total of 18,372 cases were registered, showing an increase of 81.9 percent. The data also stated maximum cases (13,814) were registered under computer related offenses (section 66 of IT Act).

The aforementioned figures are marker of gross violations of cyberspace security in India. These figures are the reported cases of criminal acts which can be understood as only the tip of an iceberg as unreported cases under the veil of ignorance, societal barriers, and fear of shame fails to come to the public eye. An increase in the recorded cases based upon annual data of 2018 and 2019, it is an encouraging news to have that awareness is rising in terms of cybercrimes. But, coming to a conclusion that only the reported cases were the only cases in India it would merely an understatement. The ripple effect of making such fallacy has huge ramifications and implications but not on a very bright side, as the stricter measures are only bound to form in any area of crime when cases have an upward and significant ascent. So, forming measures based upon data can prove to be a double-edged sword as the measures so formed may or may not represent the true picture of the demography or any strata of population.

VICTIMIZATION OF WOMEN IN CYBER SPACE:

Cyberworld is an ideal platform for gender parity as anyone from any sociological, economic, or demographic background has an ease of access to it but ironically, women are more prone to become the target of any evil act performed over internet compared to its counterpart. The reasons may differ from one societal setup to another as women have always been subjected to crime in real world, be it, rape, infanticide, trafficking, prostitution, and plethora of such sinister acts. So, in virtual world as well the plight of real world is reflected when women become acquainted with acts like, cyberbullying, pornography, picture morphing, violation of privacy, and grooming. The woe of women is thus escalated when they deal with mentioned real world and virtual world's impediments towards living a secured life which is a constitutional obligation towards every citizen of the country.

Whenever women are victimized based on afore listed premises, not only their integrity is grossly violated but it also puts a blot on the functionaries responsible for maintaining the sanctity of constitutional fundamental guidelines to provide everyone with safe and secure life and virtual experience too which is in line with mentioned articles of constitution.

❖ *Pointers describing the victimization of women in India –*

- Societal setup, i.e., patriarchal in nature especially in India,
- Lack of Women empowerment, and,
- Ignorance of the laid-out provisions for cyberspace security,
- Socio-economic factors,
- An act of revenge by snubbed suitors,

SOCIETAL SETUP IN INDIA:

Like any other society, Indian society has its own set of predefined principles and customs on which its foundation is based upon. And the very instrumental element of Indian society is its patriarchal setup which can be inferred from the myriad of cases that comes into light or gets overshadowed of child marriage, dowry, sati, abandonment of widows from society, and infanticide of female fetus. Not only the criminal cases that happens against women gives the idea of male dominance in our society but sex ratio, literacy rate, political representation and low representation in other important institutions of country speaks for itself the predicament of women in our social setup. The very concept of patriarchal structure theorizes the toxic masculinity where women have no say and are more prone to be a subject of sexual offences, domestic violence, mental anxiety and other heinous offences. And from this state of women in India they are the most vulnerable section of society to be taken as a soft target for cybercrimes. The consequences of cybercrimes inflicts so much atrocity to women's state of mind that it even leads to abetment to suicide. In a world of growing awareness about human rights such cases still need to find their place as almost majority of them aren't reported on account of the resistances that society imposes.

Lack of Women Empowerment and Ignorance of the laid-out Provisions-

Women Empowerment is an important component of a developed society where no inequality exists pertaining to gender biasness and women are treated as equal in terms of opportunities and their role in society. Empowerment of women thus plays a vital role in determining the rate of victimization of women in any society, as more aware they are about the legal recourses they can take, they are much less likely to become the prey of cybercriminals. In India, awareness about cybercrimes provisions is not much infiltrated in the minds of people as not much emphasis is given on digital literacy except for the modus operandi that is handed over either in official websites of IT ministry or through other similar official channel which makes the releases much shrouded to the general population especially women, as they lag behind in literacy holistically, let alone be the digital one. Lack of awareness among masses about the cybercrime and the legal rights of the makes the situation more favorable for the offender. Although, internet services might have reached every door today but awareness about its misuse and the online crimes still remain untouched.

Socio – Economic Factors

The socio -economic factor has an important role to play in the structure of any society. In our Indian society the socio – economic difference is totally gender based, where man is at liberty to enjoy all economic benefits and the females are deprived of this right. The patriarchal setup makes it more difficult for women to step out of the customary binding rules and have no say in economic sphere. Some studies (**Kishor and Johnson, 2004**) show that women from the poorest quintile are more likely to suffer violence than those in wealthier quintiles. In India, parental wealth is positively correlated with violence against women, as men may use violence as a tool for extracting resources, in addition to the initial dowry (**Bloch & Rao, 2002**)[27]. The male dominating society thus can be ascertained as prudent when it comes to economic liberty of women. In India we have certain societies such as Khap panchayats which prohibits the use of any electronic devices by female section of society. These unethical moral principles led to victimization of women in the real as well as virtual world.

---

[27] Cybercrime against women in India, *available at : https://ncrb.gov.in* (last visited on May 29, 2021)

An Act of Revenge by Snubbed Suitors:

Internet has emerged as a space to limitless information and a tool to serve society as a lighthouse of positive outcomes/changes through that information. But it can become a lethal space too when its outreach is used to spread compromising media with the internet users in the name of revenge, vengeance and envy. And, in majority of cases, it is seen that women are targeted as a prime victim for picture morphing, leaked sexual conversations with their partners at some point of time, hacking of personal account with a motive to defame the modesty of woman concerned and other number of abuses that happens over online platforms just to satiate the personal grudge. Such kind of violence on social media leads to extreme mental agony for women. About 20 per cent of cybercrime victims are forced to shut down their online accounts. Thus, this reflects the concern over women security in the cyber world.

1.9 IMPACT OF CYBER CRIME ON WOMEN AND SOCIETY -

Any crime that happens in our society has two facets, one which has appearance and is tangible enough to decide the course of punishment to the accused, and another one is the intangible aspect from which only the victim of that crime goes through for which no action of law has a solution to, i.e., harm to personal well-being, a monstrous perspective of humans in general, cynical attitude towards society and uncountable outcomes that crime has on person's outlook. Crime in every sense is a curse for overall development of an individual and society as a whole. Though we have legal framework set out to eliminate crime from our society and make it a better place to live. But the impact which an offence has on an individual or on society need to be taken into consideration. Criminologists and the legal experts usually analyze the ill effect that an offence have on the victim and how they perceive it in their life. Today crime has become an inseparable part of human existence and no one is untouched from the negative impact it has on the victimized person.

In this sense, cyber crime holds no exception too as it also has enlisted negative ramifications on women particularly and on society, viz –

1.) Psychological impact on the victim
2.) Impact on social and personal life of the victim
3.) Impact on Society at large
4.) Occurrence of biases and prejudices
5.) Threat to Privacy and on constitutionally guaranteed provisions
6.) Inadvertent creation of morally depraved society
7.) Hamstringing of ethics and value-based code of conduct
8.) Rise of Misogynistic thought process in concerned and around place of crime
   - Galvanization of crimes against women
   - Causing of a ripple effect furthering deterioration of standard norms of society

1.) PSYCHOLOGICAL IMPACT ON THE VICTIM –

Violence in any form has a long-lasting effect on the personality of the victim. It not only causes physical injury but even leads to impairment of mental status of the victimized person. According to some research conducted on impact of violence on women suggests that abused women in any form encounter enormous psychological suffering due to violence. At present internet is serving as a mode to commit violence against women and exploit their well-being, thus, having a far-reaching negative impact on them. Psychological impact on the victim of cybercrime, particularly, women is alarmingly worse vis-a-vis to the nation having patriarchal setup of society. In India, women face dire consequences of such acts committed on cyberspace, viz, it hurts their esteem and confidence so bad that they feel hesitant to speak about their plight aloud due to the fear of being judged in a way that put them in the bad light. This non-expression of woe or predicament being suffered by women causes number of psychological illnesses i.e., depression, anxiety, stress, and sometimes these discrepancies in mental being leads one to reach the extreme and commit suicide too. Such crimes on cyber space like image morphing, circulation of compromising media file of women, and hacking of personal account on social media to misuse the profile and defame the person causes one to go through agonizing state that deeply scars the conscious of a person and has repercussions that lasts as long as the said person's life. While to suicide rate among women, especially the one who are subjected to violence is rising at an alarming rate. In a nutshell, gruesome acts on internet harming anyone in anyone not only create turmoil in one's public life but also shakes the personal life all throughout too. Thus, it is important to have services for such victims which deals especially with such cases only and helps the victim to get out of quagmire of psychological suffering as an outcome of cruel acts on internet against anyone.

2. IMPACT ON SOCIAL AND PERSONAL LIFE OF VICTIM

Violence against women in cyberspace has a direct impact on their social and personal lifestyle. Crime committed online against women is getting graver day by day, thus, making it difficult for the users especially women and young girls to escape from the trap of offender. Cybercrimes against women is more likely be committed to sexually exploit the women and outraging her modesty. The Publishing of obscene material on internet depicting subjugated women, brings disrepute to her image in society and this makes her more vulnerable to face violence even outside. Due to patriarchal mindset of our society, it makes difficult for the victimized women to raise her voice and usually they are suppressed by the prevailing norms in our society. Instead of supporting the victimized women, the society blame her and this traumatizes her more. The impact of cybercrime against women worsened the personal life of the victim. Many instances are being reported where the snubber suitor tend to defame the victim online by publishing illicit content about her, and sharing it with users. Thus, straining their personal relationship with family and friends, which might even take form of domestic violence and subject the victim to suffer more pain.

3. IMPACT ON SOCIETY AT LARGE –

Societal aspect is another aspect that is vital and important to be studies in the cases of cybercrime. Cybercrimes relating with privacy breaches, hacking, and others creates apprehensions regarding internet usage and security it serves to the users. When a crime is committed in a society it largely effects the social setup. Due to internet anonymity in cyberspace the offender breaks all the security glasses which might protect women in society, but in cyberspace it's easy to target the victim and harass them mentally and physically usefulness of it can be ignored and thus creating an infamous name for such a vital platform of this century. Therefore, cyberspace needs strong and uncompromising regulations so as to protect the users trust and confidence while sharing any information or using any service. These regulations solely in strict implementation can fumigate the internet environment from such hackers or miscreants taking the liberty of using internet for granted and will help too to reinforce trust and confidence among users as they use this pertinent source of information.

4. OCCURRENCE OF BIASES AND PREJUDICES –

Cybercrimes especially victimizing women harms the societal view of them too. In a technologically unsound areas where any story published on internet is taken as universal truth can create severe hostility to the said person mentioning him/her in a bad light. It can thus further to an extent where violent crime or vigilantism starts happening with that person due to bias or prejudiced opinion formed over the internet without inferring the veracity of the post referred. When a crime is committed against women and it goes unreported, the offender gets another opportunity to harass the victim again in future. Although, such reports are not unusual to pop up in the newspapers that hostility was committed against someone due to public forming a strong position by referring some fabricating mouthpiece over the internet. Not this but intentional posts on the internet made solely to incite violence is also not an uncommon appearance. Many fake agendas are fueled and given mileage to so as to create discord in society by certain miscreants to solve their ulterior motives mostly harmful to general public at large. Thus, it is highly essential to have a tool that automatically check the veracity of stated information in order to completely rule out the possibility of violence being instigated against any person, institution or community as a whole.

5. THREAT TO PRIVACY AND ON CONSTITUTIONALLY GUARANTEED PROVISIONS-

It is the most rudimental and relevant question regarding cybercrimes that what happens to constitutionally guaranteed provision when such privacy breaches happen over the internet which has rather become a new normal as such news frequently hits the newspapers these days. Our data that is provided with immense trust on various sites by us when gets public by the act of hackers, privacy or right to privacy becomes a huge bone of contention. Such criminal acts deprive one of fundamental rights bestowed on him/her by our sacrosanct constitution. But, the justice in such cases is not served to the citizens as most of the times either hackers are not traced or even if they not much information in such matters is disclosed by the affected sites to save their business and reputation built on users' trust and confidence, which businesses does not want to put on the line by any means. Hence, it becomes a classic case of putting the deeds under the carpet to stay committed to the vulturous goal of businesses to earn profit at the cost of anything, be it users' trust, privacy or confidence they impose.

6. CREATION OF MORALLY INADVERTENT DEPRAVED SOCIETY-

In a way, the act of cybercrime does affect the morals and ethics upon the premises of which the societal fabric has been formed. Cybercrimes targeting women specifically, in a multifold way replicates the reality and can boost the cybercriminal's audacity to extort sexual favors on the grounds of blackmailing and using the compromising media file as a quid pro quo for such depraved arrangement. In many contemporary cases it was a common sight that compromising media was used to hush the victim and silence the voice of said person to make him mute spectator to the wrongs which such criminals are mostly inclined to and inflict on their unfortunate targets. Such incidents if comes to limelight or not but has become a sad reality which has depleted the cultural and social fabric, in return which has led to becoming of a society filled with gross violations as a new norm. Thus, the immoral society ultimately leads to a society where malicious practices get more often and the right of an individual is violated without any fear of law. This situation gives an easy hand to the like-minded people to create violence against the weaker section of our society especially the male counterpart, subjecting them to sexual harassment and mental torture.

7. HAMSTRINGING OF ETHICS AND VALUE-BASED CODE OF CONDUCT –

Cybercrimes corrupts the society on so many levels that it will become a long-winded account if all the related aspects are referred. But in general, the impact it has on youth is worth a concern as internet is a familiar tool for them nowadays and if they do not hold ethical values in them which sadly is a case in today's times, their presence on internet inevitably creates a jeopardizing situation as they are increasingly subjected to get information about anything and everything that can stimulate them to practice that knowledge impulsively and lack of ethics will create a good recipe to land them in the lap of troubles and ambit of hostile acts and bent of mind. Thus, it is a necessary evil to keep a supervision on the access of information which youth gets their fragile age as their resourceful energy if channeled otherwise has a potential to spread evil in the society in an uncontrollable manner.

8. RISE OF MISOGYNISTIC THOUGHT PROCESS IN CONCERNED AND AROUND PLACE OF CRIME –

Cybercrimes exclusively targeting women makes their existence on internet vulnerable and especially in youth when they are unaware of the consequences of their impulses when they use internet with vengeful intent and intent to outrage women's modesty, they as a byproduct forms a misogynistic outlook in their personality. It has wide repercussions, as the attitude one forms in his early ages outlasts the phase in which one forms such convictions. Domestic violence, crimes against women, toxic masculinity are just some of the phenomena which are direct consequence of misogyny among men. Sometimes, when this misogynistic orientation takes a bigger form, it is represented by society in various parameters, as sex ratio becoming non-uniform, fetus determination, preference towards boy-child and deterioration of women's value in society. Therefore, it becomes significant to save women on cyberspace from gender specific targeting and giving them a safe and reliable platform to express themselves in an unrestricted way. Also, it is vital to check the women hating ideology in young men through how they express themselves on cyberspace, to proactively trigger the attitude towards women and counter it with effective interventions.

The consequences arising out of violence which is committed against women has a deep impact on the victim and the society as a whole. Crime either committed in the physical world or in cyberspace has a significant repercussion on the social and moral perspective of every society. The emergence of online world has paved a way for more aggressive and dangerous criminal acts which are carried out against women and young girls in particular, thus, hampering their personal and mental health. This not only effect individual but also creates unrest in the society resulting into rampant violence, disturbing peace in society. Therefore, need for proper rules and regulations to eliminate the social evil of violence from occurring in the cyber space against women arises. Moreover, a proper rehabilitation mechanism is also required in order to provide aid and assistance to those victims, who suffer from ill- mental health issues resulting due to the violence omitted against them in the cyber world. It is important that we have a proper legal mechanism to eliminate exploitation of women in cyber world and instead use online platform for their upliftment in our patriarchal and male dominant society.

1.10 EVOLUTION OF CYBER CRIME

Crime is said to be a social as well as an economic phenomenon. The history of crime is as old as human society. Thus, it's a myth only if we think of a crimeless society. Ever since the dawn of human civilization, crime has been a matter of concern for the society. Historically, the concept of crime has been evolving with the passage of time and according to the change in societal setup. Some jurists are of the opinion that in earlier times only those acts were considered as criminal act which were committed against the state and it included crimes of treason, theft and spying.[28] Later on, the definition of crime changed with the passage of time, and it was not just limited to state only, rather it recognized an act to be criminal which an individual commit against the other individual. These included crime against other human such as assault, grievous hurt, rape, murder, etc.

Crime in any form cannot be justified to be right as it adversely affects all the members of society. In developing economies, more focus is on digitalization of economies and every working sector and this has directly increased cybercrime at rapid strides. Due to the huge penetration of technology in almost every walk of societal affairs right from our daily lifestyle to corporate governance and state administration, we find computers and other electronic devices have become an important part of human life. The penetration of these gadgets is so extensive that humans are now highly addicted to it.

Today internet is the ever growing fastest technology which has made human lifestyle easy and comfortable. It has various benefits for mankind like fast and easy communication, online shopping, online movie and songs downloads, online transactions, online business and trade, instant messaging and fast searching engine which has great impact on our day-to-day lifestyle. But the internet has also served as a platform for various cybercrimes that takes place in virtual world. Different kinds of internet scams and frauds are taking place in the virtual space and it is important that one needs to be very careful while sharing any kind of confidential information with stranger, as they could use the same against the user to commit cybercrime. Ever since the internet services was introduced, the victimization of the internet user is something that has been bothering individuals and the corporate world at large.

It is rightly said that technological development in every area is likely to bring a drastic change in every walk of life. Thus, due to scientific and technological advancement, especially in the field of communication and information network have created great havoc by opening new dimension for criminal activities. Cyber-crimes are committed with the assistance of internet and cell phones. Cybercrimes includes all sort of criminal activities done with the help of computers , by having unauthorized access to the personal information of other person which further perpetuates crimes such as : crimes related to economy, sale of illegal articles, pornography, online gambling, intellectual property crime, e-mail, spoofing, forgery, cyber defamation, cyberstalking ,cyber harassment ,virus attacks, gender based

---

[28] *Supra 2 168*

crimes, theft of information contained in the electronic form, e-mail bombing, morphing etc. All such acts of crime will come under the broader definition of cybercrime.

DEVELOPMENT OF CYBER CRIME IN RECENT TIMES:

In present time Information and communications technologies (ICT) has become a part of everyone's life and this is visible with the rapid growth of Internet and emergence of social networking sites in cyber space. With the ever-growing trend of ICT, it has thus become an indispensable function of commerce and government. However, the Internet has also become a "double-edged sword" in the hands of perpetrators. Along with internet convenience and advantages comes the inconvenience of computer related crimes. The Internet was originally built for research findings and to make work easy but eventually this forum turned out to be a safer place for perpetrators to carry out crimes. Lack of awareness among masses makes it easy for perpetrator to harass the user. The rapid evolution of the computer networks and internet services provided a gateway for the offenders to harass the victim at ease. [29]

The main idea behind inventing internet service was to carry out research work, but later on it changed from a search engine to a platform of various networking sites. This rampant advancement has raised the concern of the states worldwide over the increasing number of cyber-attacks that takes place every second. Apparently, gender-based crimes are getting more enhanced with new technology advancement. Women and young children are becoming victim to cyber offences and are being exploited at large. Cyber space is becoming a place which is quite often used by the criminals to exploit women and young children to seek revenge or to gain monetary benefit from them. India is the third largest internet user in the world after U.S.A and China. Thus, this poses a great risk for increase in crimes which result in addition to the prevailing crime rate in our country.

To combat the menace of ever-increasing digital crimes it is the need of the hour to have efficient legal framework dealing with such crimes. In this regard various states have formulated laws to regulate the activities of its citizens and the business firms in cyber space

---

[29] *Supra 24 1*

and has enhanced the cyber security channels to further stop these attacks and safeguards the interest of individual even in virtual world. India is no exception to it, as there is surge in the cases of cyber-attacks in India also. In order to combat the menace of cybercrime various legislation has been enacted by the government. There are many acts regulating the conduct of persons online and punishes the offender who violates these laws. One such important statutes enacted by the Indian Government is the Information Technology Act ,2000 which regulated the cyber-attacks against the internet service users. Additionally, certain amendments were made in the Indian Penal Code, to safeguard the interest of women in the society and even in cyber space.

1.11 LEGAL FRAMEWORK SAFEGUARDING THE INTEREST OF WOMEN IN CYBER SPACE

Crime against women has been there in our society from time immemorial and to eradicate the old age norm of subjecting women to violence has been the priority of every state. While the technology advancement has somehow brought a change in our society and broad-minded approach has been adopted by the society where rights of women have gained a momentum. For instance, the Metoo# moment in the virtual world swept worldwide attention, where women from every walk of life shared their incidence of violence in the society. There is no doubt that technology has a revolutionary change in our societal aspect, but it even brings with it the menace of cyber crime committed in the dark space of cyber world. The dark web in the cyberspace has enhanced the spectrum of crime and violent act committed against women in particular in the cyber world.

Cybercrime against women has emerged as a major concern for the law enforcing agencies. India being the third largest country in the world to avail the internet services is not immune to cyber -attacks. The rapid advancement of technology and coming up of social media platform is becoming a tool for subjecting women and young girls to cyber violence. Cyber offence such as cyber defamation, sextortion, identity theft, blackmailing, publishing obscene images of women, cyber harassment, cyber voyeurism, bullying, cyber trafficking of women, etc. are some of the common offences committed in cyberspace against women. In India, we have some laws and special statues which are especially framed, by keeping women rights in mind. The Indian Criminal Justice System has some provisions enlisted in the statute which preserve rights of the women and protect them against any violence. Moreover, the Constitution of India further enlist some provisions which protect women from any kind of violence.

When it comes to eliminating crime against women in cyber space, it might get complicated and difficult to completely eradicate its menace. But it becomes necessary to protect interest of every user. Article 14, Article 15, Article 21 and Article 23-24, promotes upliftment of women in our society by bestowing certain rights on them and punishes the one who infringes their rights. Its usage is applicable even in the cyber world, whereby anyone who have criminal tendency to commit crime against women shall be held accountable for his act and penalized for the same. In addition to these aforementioned provisions, the Indian Criminal Justice system especially Indian Penal Code, 1860 and Code of Criminal Procedure Code ,1973 also protects interest of women and safeguard their rights in consonance with the constitutional provisions.

Furthermore, various amendments have been made in the prevailing statues to protect the women against cyber violence. There are number of acts which enumerate special provisions to regulate the misbehavior of an individual against women and prescribe harsh punishment for such offender. The Central Government has enacted some important statues which work in the direction of removing disparities in the society by giving rights to women and preserving their dignity in the cyber space and includes:

- The Information Technology Act, 2000
- The Immoral Trafficking (Prevention) Act of 1956
- The Indecent Representation of Women (Prohibition) Act, 1986
- The Protection of Children Against Sexual Offences (POCSO) Act, 2012
- The Criminal Amendment Act of 2013
- The Personal Data Protection Bill, 2019

Apart from the above-mentioned statutes, the Indian Judiciary has played a major role in defining the role of government to protect the women in cyber space and passed out certain judgements which sets out to be precedent for future. Judiciary being an independent body of the democratic setup of India has significantly worked in the direction of promoting women empowerment in our society and preserved their basic rights in the virtual space. The Indian Legislation and Judiciary is working forward to curb the ever-increasing menace of cybercrime against women and young girl child. Although, there are statues protecting the women users from falling into wrong hands, but still there remains lacunae in our legal system to regulate the conduct of private companies and other sources responsible for violation of women rights in cyber space.

1.12 LITERATURE REVIEW

1. The Constitution of India [30]

Article 14, Article 15(3), Article 21 and other relevant Articles:

Article 14 embodies the general principles of equality before law and equal protection of laws.

The state shall not deny to ANY PERSON, EQUALITY BEFORE LAW (negative obligations)

AND EQUAL PROTECTION OF LAWS (positive in nature) "within the territory of India".

The general principle held that equal protection of law means the right to equal treatment of every individual in similar circumstances. The word reasonable means "the classification should not be arbitrary but must be rational and justified one".

The classical test which judiciary enunciated requires the fulfillment of two conditions:

The classification must be founded on "intelligible differentia" which distinguishes those who are grouped together from others. And the differential must have a rational relation to the object achieved by the law under challenge.

---

[30] Narender Kumar, *Constitutional Law of India 110* (Allahabad Law Agency, Haryana 9th edn. 2015)

☐ *In Deputy Inspector of Police vs. S Samuthiram* (2012) [31]eve- teasing in any form is violation of Article 14 and 15 of the Constitution: In this case the court observed that eve-teasing in any form is a violation of women dignity which is protected under Article 21. It is a sex-based discrimination against womanhood which violate article 14 and 15 of constitution. Equality is a dynamic concept in nature which cannot be cribbed, cabined and confined. Where an act Is arbitrary, it is implicit in it that it is unequal both according to political logic and constitutional law and is therefore violation of Article 14" *Said by Justice Bhagwati in E.P. Royappa vs. State of Tamil Nadu.*

Article 15 (3) empowers state to create special provisions for protecting the interest of women and children.

In Dattatray vs. State of Bombay A.I.R 1953 it was observed that clause 3 provides power to state to enact such laws which strengthen and improves the status of women in society.

Article 21: Protection of Life and Personal Liberty

A person shall not be deprived of his life or personal liberty except according to procedure established by law. This Article guarantees right to live with liberty and dignity. If anyone infringes this right or injures dignity of some person, he shall be subjected to punishment according to procedure established by law.

Article 21 also provides for right to privacy as a fundamental right of an individual.

☐ In K.S. Puttaswamy vs. Union of India (2017) the Supreme Court held that the right to privacy is protected as a fundamental constitutional right under Article 14, 19 and 21 of Indian Constitution.[32]

2. Cyber Laws in the Information Technology Act 2000

Information Technology Act of 2000 lay down certain provisions which provides safeguard for women against cybercrimes. It defines the various cyber offences committed against women in cyber space and prescribe penalty in this regard as per the nature of offence.

---

[31] A.I.R 2012
[32] A.I.R 2017

3. Indian Penal Code, 1860

The Indian Penal Code is the main postulate of the Indian Criminal Justice System. It consists of a list which enumerates various offences committed against human being and prescribe the punishments for a particular illegal act. IPC lays down various acts which the law considers illegal and against human being and provides punishment for every such act. It covers wide range of sections which are inserted particularly to prevent victimization of women and secure their interest by punishing those who commit violence against them.

4. Immoral Trafficking (Prevention) Act of 1956

The domestic legislation which deals which the prevention of trafficking in women and importation of girls from other nations is knowns as Immoral Trafficking (Prevention) Act of 1956. The present statute deals with trafficking of women in the real world or through cyber space and prescribe the amount of penalty and fine in relation to committing the offence of buying and selling women for monetary benefit. It even recognizes the act of commercial prostitution where women are forced into flesh trade as a criminal offence and prescribe punishment for the same.

5. Indecent Representation of Women (Prohibition) Act, 1986

The present statue lays down rules and regulations in order to avoid indecent representation of women either through online mode, magazines, advertisement, pamphlets or on social networking sites. The prohibits such acts which brings disrepute to a women dignity in the society and preserve her right to life and liberty.

6. The Protection of Children from Sexual Offences (POCSO) ACT,2012

It is one of the important legal statute of Indian criminal justice system which was especially enacted to protect the children from sexual exploitation. It lays down stringent provisions to inflict harsh punishment on the offender who exposes the child to any sexual offense or use them for commercial sexual trade. It protects the young children from being sexually exploited on the web and safeguard their primary interest. The POCSO Act, lays down provisions which define the offences and prescribe punishment for the same. It punishes the offender to carry out sexual harassment of cyber pornography against young child especially young girls who are more prone to be victimized and sexually harassed.

7. Cyber Laws in the Information Technology Age

By: Karnika Seth

Published by: Lexis Nexis

It is a comprehensive work that aptly highlights new laws, policies, cases, concept, events and studies that have evolved cyber law in the national and international spheres. It discusses landmark cases, including Shreya Singhal vs. Union of India, which struck down Section 66A of the IT ACT OF 2000 as unconstitutional. Another landmark case was Anwar vs. P.K. Basheer which clarified the relevance of electronic evidence in India. In this paper it has been observed that with the increase in use of technology the cybercrime is also rising.

8. Legal Dimensions of Cyberspace

By: Raman Mittal

Published by: Indian law Institute

The book discusses various laws that are applicable to cyberspace. It elucidates legal framework for commerce, contracts, intellectual property protection, privacy rights and crimes in cyberspace. The book is divided into three parts-Part I deals with Intellectual Property protection in cyber world, Part II deals with E-Commerce including online contracts between parties and their protection and Part III deals with the Cyber World particularly in context to the Information Technology Act 2000 viz.-the Computer Crimes, Cyber Privacy and protection against cybercrimes.

9. Information Technology

By: Vakul Sharma

Published by: Universal Law Publishing

This book captures the essence of the Information Technology Act 2000.This book provides in depth information about the IT Act and the defects in its implication in practicality. Issues related to cyber-crime, virtual terrorism, encryption, digital India, social media, cyber security have been discussed in the legal context. Further, considering the nature of the subject and the international perspective this book includes a comparative analysis of corresponding provisions in other jurisdiction to render an in- depth view to readers.

10 'CYBER CRIME AGAINST WOMEN IN INDIA 'by Debarati Halder, K. Jaishankar (2017) analyzed various cybercrimes against women in India which are very much prevalent nowadays. It discusses cybercrimes against women in India, various forms of online crimes including hate speeches, trolling, cyber bullying, online grooming, infringement of privacy and sexual offences on internet and other social media platform. In this book the above-mentioned crimes are discussed in detailed and provides for preventive measures in order to combat the cybercrimes against women. The scholar identified the factors associated behind the causation of cybercrime against women in India. The study revealed that there is no uniform law to combat the cybercrimes against women but instead we are having scattered laws embodied in traditional criminal laws such as Indian Penal Code (IPC), the Evidence Act or the latest Information Technology Act of 2000 for providing justice to the victims. Furthermore, it has been noted that many websites have their servers outside India and harassers take huge advantage of this.[33]

11. Victimization of Women Beneath Cyberspace in India published in article section of Manupatra by Monika Jain. This research study provides a review and analyses of the development of regulatory instruments statutes, recommendations and guidelines in order to protect privacy and related interests of women in cyberspace. This paper presents a predictive analysis of cybercrime against women in India and laws that present cybercrime victimization in general and women especially. [34]

---

[33] 6 Debarati Halder and K. Jaishankar, CYBER CRIME AGAINST WOMEN IN INDIA (Sage Publications, Mathura Road (New Delhi)
[34] Victimization of Women Beneath Cyber Space in India, available at: www.manupatra.com (last visited on 24

12. **Violence Against Women in Cyber World**: A Special Reference to India published in 'International Journal of Advanced Research in Management and Social Sciences' (ISSN:2278-6236) by Jaspreet.

This research paper discusses that the violence against women is a violation of human rights and not a new phenomenon. It is always taking its shape from time to time in Indian history. With the passage of time, many feminist leaders fought for violence against women and for their empowerment in the society, but there is no end of her vulnerable life and her exploitation. This paper presumes the cyber violence against women, how it is impacting their social life in context to India. It highlights the reasons and forms of cybercrimes and explores some suggestions how to curb cybercrime against women. The main postulate of the paper is that the Indian women are still not open to immediately report the cyber abuse or cyber-crime. The biggest problem of cybercrime lies in the modus operandi and the motive of the cyber-criminal. Cyber space is a transit space for many people, including offenders. Any person may come and go. This provides an opportunity to the offender to escape after commission of cybercrime. An efficient mechanism is required to combat such situation and keep a check over such cyber activities.

13. **Women Harassment in Digital Space in India,** published in "International Journal of Pure and Applied Mathematics "(ISSN: 1314-3395) by Shweta Sankar.

This paper discusses about the impact of digitalization in India and how far it has contributed towards women harassment in cyber world. It gives a detailed view about how women in India are subjected to cybercrimes and its impact on their social relations. In its ambit the scholar has discussed about why the cybercrime against women are less reported even after so many incidences taking place daily. This paper studies about various methods used by cyber criminals in order to harass women in cyber space.

14.**Big Data Privacy**: A Technological Perspective and Review Published at scholarly by Priyanka Jain, Mansi Aggarwal and Nilay Khar. This research papers critically analyze the use of privacy in the business transaction and daily online work. It gives a brief insight about various privacy preserving mechanism which is developed for protecting the privacy of every individual in cyber space at every stage for example data generation, data storage and data processing. The paper presents recent techniques used to prevent privacy infringement and preserve the data in computer devices. It further discusses the importance of cyber security and its relevance while dealing with privacy in cyberspace.[35]

15. Indian Women at Risk in the Cyberspace: A Conceptual Model of Reasons of Victimization, published in International Journal of Cyber Criminology "(ISSN:0974-2891)"by Tanya Saha:

This research paper gives an insight about the reasons behind victimization of women in the cyber space and the long-lasting negative impact it has on the victimized women. It gives a detailed account of various factors which has significantly led to victimization of women in cyber space. This paper gives a whole idea about main factors such as easy accessibility of internet services, the patriarchal mindset of people, lack of knowledge about computer and computer related offences and the addiction of internet, which has contributed a lot in carrying out criminal acts against women at large. This paper discusses about the abovementioned factors which are of major concern as it has far reaching impact on over all growth of women in a society.

16.Cybercrime against women: A gloomy outlook of Technological Advancement by Abhinav Sharma and Ajay Singh:

In this research paper, the author has scrutinized the role of increased technological advancement, and increasing trend of internet usage and social media sites which are the major cause of increasing cyber-crime cases against women in Indian Society. The paper also discusses the role of legislation and judiciary in regulating the increase of cyber offences against women and how far have we achieved it.[36]

17. Privacy in India in The Age of Big Data

---

[35] Bid data privacy: A technological perspective and review, available at: *https://journalofbigdata.springeropen.com* (last visited on May 30, 2021)
[36] Cybercrime against women: A Gloomy Outlook of Technological Advancement, available at: *https://www.ijlmh.com* (last visited on May 30, 2021)

Written By: Buddhadeb Halder

Published By: Digital Empowerment Foundation

This research paper discusses how the concept of big data has emerged with the technological advancement and the issue of Privacy infringement associated with it. It defines a relationship that is established between data and the privacy. It gives a brief account of how data is being transferred from one device to another and raising concern of protection of privacy of the users.

18. Right to Privacy in Digitalized India, published in International Journal of Pure and Applied Mathematic "(ISSN: 1314-3395)" by Santhosh S and Ms. Renuga C

This paper specifically focusses on right to privacy of internet users in digitalized India and its impact on the citizens. It discusses the impact that digitalized India has on their privacy. With the advent of internet and everything getting digitalized has immensely led to data breach in the cyberspace leading to cybercrimes taking place against the users.

19. Cyberspace and Women, published in International Journal of Engineering and Advanced Technology (IJEAT)(ISSN:2249-8958) by Mayur U. Pawar and Archana Sakure

The paper discusses the major reasons for the growth of cyber violence against women in the era of cyber socialization. This paper recognizes the common types of cyber offences committed against women namely cyber stalking, cyber pornography, circulating indecent images or video of females, morphing, blackmailing or threatening, trolling and bullying. The paper analyzes each component which leads to victimization of women in cyberspace and highlights various cases involving cybercrimes against women.

20. Cyber Trafficking: Recruiting Victims of Human Trafficking Through the Net

It gives a proper gist about how cyberspace has become a platform to carry illegal human trafficking online. Trafficking of women for sex-labor, young girls, trafficking of organs and mail order brides are some of the major forms of cyber-trafficking. From the moment the traffickers have got easy access to internet services, they have been using cyberspace as mode for carrying cyber-trafficking. Thus, it is necessary to curb its menace and this paper focus on the aspect of cyber-trafficking and need for international treaties to eliminate such offence.[37]

21. The Emergence of Cyber Activity as a Gateway to Human Trafficking

The paper defines the concept of cyber trafficking in cyber space and how victims are being targeted online. The use of internet and cyberspace has made a huge contribution in human trafficking of women and young girls. It gives brief account of various legislation passed around the globe to stop the human trafficking in cyber space and make it a far better place to interact.[38]

22. Cyber Violence Against Women and Girls -UNESCO

The report has been written in order to draw a collective attention of world towards the plight of women and young girls who are sexually abused in cyber space. This report is presented by UNESCO to bring into notice the violence against women which is meted on them in virtual world.[39]

23. Present scenario of cybercrime in INDIA and its preventions, published in International Journal of Science and Engineering Research (ISSN: 2229-5518) By Shubham Kumar and Uday Kumar

This research paper tries to explain the expanding use of internet services in India and the impact of cyber crime in our society. It aims at describing various legislative provisions incorporated in our criminal justice system in order to prevent cases of cyber crimes in future. It elaborates various sections of Information Technology Act, 2000 and the importance of

---

[37] Cyber Trafficking : Recruiting Victims of Human Trafficking Through The Net , available at : *https://crime-in-crisis.com* (last visited on June 3, 2021)
[38] The Emergence of Cyber Activity as a Gateway to Human Trafficking, available *at* : *https://blogs.bu.edu* (last visited on June 2 , 2021)
[39] Cyber Violence Against Women and Girls -UNESCO, *available at:* *https://en.unesco.org* (last visited on June 3, 2021)

The Protection of Personal Data Bill, 2019 which prevents breach of data in cyberspace and avoid cybercrime to some extent.

24. Womens Right in India:

By: Dr. Radhika Kapur

The paper lays down emphases on women rights which are guaranteed by the Indian Constitution and other legal statutes incorporated for women empowerment in our society. Violation against women in present society has turned to be more heinous and graver in nature, and thereby, it becomes the duty of legislation to protect women against any abuse or harassment. Therefore, in INDIA we have number of statutes which protects women interest and try to eliminate the prejudice held by the society women are slave to men. This paper work in the direction of providing a proper insight about laws that help in curbing violence against women.

1.13 PROBLEM PROFILE

In the current era of globalization, we see that technological advancement has brought a revolutionary change in our lifestyle. One such development that has brought a revolutionary change in our society comes with enhancing internet services and making it easily available to each and every individual. Today, internet has become our way of living and life without internet is unimaginable. We are completely dependent on internet in order to carry out our daily routine work. The cyber development might have made our life easy but it has paved a way for "Cyber Crime".

Cybercrime is a new way of committing crime online in cyberspace. It has become a new way to carry all sorts of illegal acts whose commission in real world was quite difficult. The cyber criminals have got a fast and cheap space to commit violence against the users for monetary gains. Among all, victimization of women in cyberspace has emerged a new phenomenon in criminology. Women are more vulnerable to be victimized in cyberspace. Violence against women and young girls in cyberspace has gained momentum in past few years with a sudden rise in rate of cybercrime against women. The most common types of cyber offences committed against women in cyberspace include- Identity theft, Cyber Fraud,

Online Grooming, Privacy Invasion, Cyber Stalking, Cyber defamation, publishing and circulating obscene images of women online, blackmailing through online mode, Pornography, sextortion, cyber-trafficking etc. The increase in number of cybercrimes against female section of our society in particular has posed a challenge to the legal framework of the nation and making it a challenging task for the government to eliminate the evil of crime against women from society.

This paper discusses the concept of cybercrime against women, why victimization of women is more common in cyber world, and reason for their victimization in virtual space and its impact on them if and the preventive measures taken up by the Government in order to stop this menace against women. Furthermore, this paper explains the role of judiciary in combating the menace of cybercrime and the challenges faced by it during adjudication of power in certain cases.

1.14 RESEARCH QUESTIONS

• What are the reasons for increase in rate of cybercrime against women?

• What are the challenges in the existing legislations mechanism in relation to cyber crimes?

against women and why the enforcement agencies are not effective to ascertain the cyber crime

against women?

• Whether the present legislations are sufficient to curb the cybercrimes against women in India?

• What is the liability of Internet service provider in relation to cyber offences?

1.15 RESEARCH METHODOLGY

The principle aim of this research paper is to critically analyze the emerging trend of cyber crime against women in particular and the legal statutes established to eradicate the instances of cyber violence committed against female section of our society. The methodology adopted in carrying out research work is based on secondary data which includes various books, magazines, encyclopedia, research paper, legal statutes, newspaper, various judgements passed by the Hon'ble Courts, various reports both published and unpublished, getting sustainable help from internet resources as well.

1.16 OBEJCTIVES OF THE STUDY

1.) To study the nature of cybercrimes against women in virtual world

2.) To study the criminal tendencies of cyber criminals and already defined legislative provisions

concerned to combat the same.

3.) To study the impact of cybercrimes on victim and on society as a whole.

4.) To delineate the reasons behind the less conviction rate in terms of cybercrimes.

5.) To identify the loopholes (if any) in the existing legal structure on cybercrimes.

6.) To establish the need for the fast-track redressal mechanism for cybercrime complaints.

1.17 TENTATIVE CHAPTERISATION

Chapter 1. Introduction

This chapter explains the definition of cybercrime and emerging trends of cyber offences in recent times. Further it talks about the reason for increasing violence against women in cyber space. It gives brief account about what cyber-crime is all about and how it has evolved with the advent of new technology. It gives a brief idea about various cyber offences committed against women around globe. Moreover, it discusses the various types of cybercrimes such as cyber fraud, e-mail related crimes, cyber stalking, data breach, privacy infringement, cyber defamation, cyber pornography, blackmailing etc. It highlights different medium used by cyber hackers in order to commit crime against women. It underlines the impact of crime committed against women in cyberworld and society as a whole.

CHAPTER 2. EVOLUTION OF CYBER CRIME

This chapter deals with the evolution of cybercrime in cyber world. Internet evolution brought a revolutionary change in the way we communicate and perceive things around us. Internet evolved from a research tools to a communicating forum where people from different part of world share their thoughts and bring cultural -integrity among all. But along with advantage comes certain repercussions and one such is Cybercrime. Online services provided a platform for the cyber criminals to carry all sort of illegal activities in the cyberspace. Cybercrime is as old as technology itself. Earlier cybercrime was committed through telephonic medium but internet made it easier and more accessible to commit crime through its various components. One such important component of cyberworld is social media, which provides detailed information about the person making it more convenient for criminals to carry out criminal activities. It gives an insight of gradual evolution of cybercrimes starting from a small platform to forming a wide chain of organized crimes.

CHAPTER 3. LEGISLATIVE PROVISIONS

This chapter gives an insight about the rules and regulations In Indian Criminal Justice System, which deals with offences committed against women and young girls in cyberspace. It deals with the legislations established to curb the cyber offences against women in particular in India.

This chapter elaborate various provisions of Indian Constitution, Indian Penal Code ,1860 an, \Information Technology Act,2000, Immoral Trafficking (Prevention) Act, 1956, POCSO Act, 2012, Indecent Representation of Women (Prohibition) Act, 1986 and the Criminal Amendment Act of 2013.which deals with safeguarding the interest of women in cyberworld. It provides a detailed account about the lacunae present in our legislation and the ineffectiveness of provisions while dealing with cases of cyber offences against women in general.

CHAPTER 4. ROLE OF JUDICIARY

This chapter provides an insight regarding the role of judiciary in combating the cybercrime against women in India. It discusses the landmark among them Ritu Kohli cases which was the first case of cyber stalking in India to be reported. The role of judiciary is of utmost importance while dealing any case in order to provide justice to the victim and punish the wrongdoer. It elaborates various judicial pronouncement made by the judicial body to combat the cyber menace against women in Indian society. Furthermore, it gives a gist about the challenges that judiciary faces while adjudicating a matter and the need to bring a change in our investigating procedure.

CHAPTER 5. DATA ANALYSEES

Under this chapter a quantitative research has been made on the number of cyber offences that has been committed against women in India from 2017-2018.It gives a detailed account of violation against women in cyberspace which took place in India state vise and the increase in number in different states.

CHAPTER 6: CONCLUSION AND SUGGESTIONS

This chapter provides for various suggestions and recommendations made after a complete research on violation against women in cyberspace and gives idea in order to combat with the cybercrimes against women to avoid further victimization of women in the hands of cyber criminals. The chapter recommends for imparting awareness about cyber offences in schools and various other institutions and establishing an efficient intelligence mechanism which easily detect the cybercrimes and provides security against any cyber threat and fraud.

EVOLUTION OF CYBER CRIME

Chapter 2

2.1 BACKGROUND

Cyber Crime is a crime that emerged simultaneously as an offshoot of internet in criminal terms or criminal dimension. Internet as an innovation happened in 1983, post which many fundamental changes happened in our society on account of various services relating to it. Be it making our lives easier to streamlining communication, internet has been instrumental in various ways which includes imparting online education, carrying online trade, bridging the gap of communication which existed prior to coming up of internet services and many more. One of the biggest contributions made by the internet services in recent times is in the e-commerce and communication sector. The emergence of Information and Communication Technology has brought a significant change in our social life in a positive manner. It has developed a mutual relationship with human lives but our over dependence on this social networking system has made us an easy target to be victimized in the reel sphere of cyber space. In past few years the rate of crime in the virtual world has increased at a fast pace thus, challenging the present legal scenario.

2.2 THE EMERGENCE OF INTERNET

The Internet in this contemporary era has revolutionized the computer and communications world like nothing before. In earlier times where the mode of dissemination of information and communication was limited, at that time the invention of the telegraph, telephone, radio, and computer set the stage for integrating the unprecedented capabilities of mankind. Among all the great inventions in the history of mankind, the internet is a world -wide broadcasting platform which serves as a medium for collaboration and interaction between individual irrespective of geographical barriers.[40]

When it comes to the most reliable and successful invention of mankind, the Internet serves as one of the most successful examples of it as it represents the benefits of sustained investment in the research and information sector. At the initial stage the use of internet was limited to research work and for government official work only but later on its usage was extended for industrial and corporate firms. In the present scenario the education sector has incorporated this new exciting technology to provide online forum to impart knowledge to everyone. T Today we live in the world of internet which is a widespread information infrastructure, the initial blueprint of what is often called the National (or Global or Galactic) Information Infrastructure. [41]Its history is complex and involves many aspects in its ambit such as – technological, organizational, and community. It has its influence in every walk of our life and its roots are not just embedded in the technical fields of computer communications but has reached throughout society.

2.2.1 HISTORICAL ACCOUNT OF INTERNET

The origins of the internet services date back to late 1950s in USA. are rooted in the USA, when the cold war was at its peak and there was a huge tension between the two most powerful allies – North America and the Soviet Union. Both of them were the superpowers at that time and were in possession of deadly nuclear weapons, and people living there were in constant fear of attacks and might face the same situation of World War once again. To avoid the World War situation in any case the US Government realized that there was a need of an effective communications system to be prepared in case that the Soviet Union carry mass destruction by nuclear attack. It was time to invent such an efficient communication system which was reliable and easy to handle, and this gave birth to Internet.[42]

- **ARPANET:**

---

[40] Brief History of Internet, *available at* ;https://www.internetsociety.org>internet> brief-history (last visited on June 4, 2021)
[41] *Ibid*
[42] A Short History of The Internet, *available at:* https://www.scienceandmediamuseum.org.uk (last visited on June 4, 2021)

ARPANET, in full Advanced Research Projects Agency Network, was an experimental computer network program that is regarded as the predecessor of the Internet. The Advanced Research Projects Agency (ARPA), was an arm of the U.S. Defense Department, that was funded and development by the Advanced Research Projects Agency Network (ARPANET) in the late 1960s. The principal mandate of it was to link the computer system at Pentagon-funded research institutions over telephone lines in order to provide a communication platform. At its initial stage ARPANET was a Wide Area Network which linked many Universities and research centers to carry their field work easily and was first to use the concept of packet switching and, therefore was a landmark stone at the beginning of what we consider the Internet world today. ARPANET was created with an aim to provide a better service program that made easier for people to access computers, and to have a more effective communication method for the military officials.[43] Later on, in late 80s it was no longer an experimental base, rather the communication facilities got enhanced and was utilized by the commerce sector at a large extent. Even today, ARPANET is considered as the backbone of internet.

- **DEVELOPMENT OF TCP/IP BASED INTERNETWORK:**

Internet official came onto existence in 1983 on 1st January. Prior to coming up of internet services, the various computer networks did not have any standard medium to communicate with each other. In late 80s a new modified version of communication protocol was established and was known as Transfer Control Protocol/Internetwork Protocol (TCP/IP). With the coming up of this version now it was possible for different kinds of computers working on different networks to "communicate" with each other. ARPANET and the Defense Data Network officially adopted the new standard of communication program of TCP/IP standard on January 1, 1983, hence the birth of the Internet. The adoption of TCP/IP now allowed to communicate with other computer system based on one universal language.[44] As the use of the TCP/IP standard was used frequently by every computer system paving way for other entire networks to interconnect and finally a better and efficient internet network was born.

---

[43] ARPANET, Definition, Map, Cold War, First Message, *available at: https://www.britanica* .com (last visited on June 4, 2021)
[44] *Ibid*

- **EMERGENCE OF WEB WORLD:**

The internet is a huge bucket of network of computer system which enables to interconnect the other computer devices with each other, but at the front foot it was the World Wide Web that brought a radical change in the technology by forming a bridge that linked information together and made it easily accessible to everyone. The essence of the world wide web is that it acts as a collection of webpages found on the network of computers –through which the browser uses the internet to access the particular page on web.

By the early 1990s, the Internet services was limited for use of defense mechanism and commercial activities. Public access to the Internet use was not there. It was in late 90s that internet expanded rapidly due to the flexible nature of the analog telephone network and the availability of modems for connecting the computers to internet network. April 1995 was memorable day in the history of communication technology where, all commercialization restrictions on the Internet were lifted up and now it was available for the public usage. Although still the primarily usage of internet was limited to academics and businesses, but in later period the internet trend was grown, with the number of hosts reaching up to 2 lakhs. But it was with the invention of Web that launched the internet to mass popularity overnight.[45] The world wide web opened up the doors of internet services to every individual and was no just limited for scientific use. It connected the world in such a way that made it much easier for people around the globe to access information, share, and communicate with people living overseas. Since then, it has allowed people around the globe to share their work and thoughts through social networking sites and has turned the globe into an integrated society.

The dimension of internet and the communication technology got evolved gradually and changed the whole perspective of the society. Moreover, with the coming up of world wide web the interface of technology changed completely. It modified the

---

[45] World Wide Web: The Invention That Connected the World, available at: https://www.artsandcultutre.google.com(last visited on June 5, 2021)

networking mode by enabling the public to have direct and easy access to internet services.

- **E-MAIL: A STEP TOWARDS BETTER COMMUNICATION**

E-mail glorification was an important step towards enhancing internet platform. It was usually used for formal and official work. This sphere was used by the students, professors, research scholars and entrepreneurs to send official work and communicate with their colleagues. It changed the whole scenario of connecting to world and carrying formal work at an ease.

2.2.2 CHANGING PATTERNS OF INTERNET IN PRESNET TIME

The widespread usage of internet has brough a conventional change in the present world. It has a constant influence in our daily walk of life. The most recent phase which completely evolved the concept of Internet has been characterized by significant and the gradual changes in the ways that people access and use the network facility. Further it got evolved by the comprehensive modes in which the foremost infrastructure of the network has evolved to cope with the changes outside the virtual world. The comprehensive development that took place in the arena of internet which entirely changed its concept came up with prominent advancement of mobile connectivity, social networking sites, expansion of e-commerce and commission of cyber offences in virtual world.[46]

- **MOBILE CONNECTIVITY:**

The landmark moment in the history of internet is marked with the invention of "smartphone" in 2007. The smartphone technology has emerged into a successful e-device for instant communication which changed the way in which we communicate with others. In the current scenario, this modern gadget turns out to be the most essential tool for all ages of people to

---
[46] Ibid

fulfil their daily task and communicate with their loved ones. It cannot be denied that this device has made a lot of progress in all spheres of communication as it's easy to use and is time saving. Most of the people use smartphones to access the internet services. According to a report published by the World Advertising Research Centre (WARC) almost three quarters (72.6 percent) of internet users will access the web solely via their smartphones by 2025, which is equivalent to nearly 3.7 billion people around the globe. The report stated that by 2025, round about 1.3 billion are going to access the internet via smartphones.[47]

The implication of the mobile connectivity especially smartphones has evolved the working of internet in cyber space. It even enhanced the advancement in the cyber space by expanding the usage of networking sites and brough a radical change in e-commerce. On an average an individual spends 3 hours scrolling on internet. Mobile connectivity has not only changed our social life but has even improved the network connectivity. Smartphone has a great influence on over all social interaction and day to day activities of its users. This hazy-crazy digital device has divided the world into a "Digi- world" where these devices has taken an edge over other traditional way of communicating and receiving information. Internet along with smart phones has a revolutionary impact on the overall development of mankind. At present one cannot imagine life without smartphone and internet connectivity.

- **SOCIAL NETWORKING SITES:**

    Looking at the present scenario of the virtual world the online networking sites have a predominance over internet services. Social media allows the users to communicate with people from around the world thus forming a relationship with users belonging to distinct backgrounds, resulting in a tenacious social structure. A noteworthy outcome of this social structure is that the upcoming generation withholds a massive amount of information than the earlier one, thus, establishing a society where people from every sect come forward and share their views. It has enabled the world to come

---

[47] Smartphones :72% of people will only use mobile for internet, available *at* : *https://saucelabs.com*(last visited on June 5, 2021)

together in order to remove the social and cultural barriers that existed prior to coming up of social networking sites. While talking about social media, applications such as Facebook, WhatsApp, Twitter, You Tube, Snapchat, Pinterest and Instagram often strikes our mind. These applications are highly influential and have direct impact on the behavior of the user. These social media applications not only serve the purpose of entertainment and communication but it has even widened the scope for carrying out business activities on this platform. Social media sites are already so deeply rooted in our daily lives that the users rely on them for every need, that range from getting updated with daily news and updates on critical events to entertainment, connecting them with family and friends, fulfill the emotional needs of users, provides an easy access to online shopping etc.

The arena of internet completely got a new look with the coming up of social media sites. Today, the use of social media sites has increased at a par, as stated by a report published in 2017 which provided a data revealing that among all, Facebook enjoys the exalted position of being the market leader of the social media world, with 1.97 billion monthly users. In addition to posts, social media sites are bombarded with photo and video uploads, and according to the recent numbers, about 400 million snaps a day have been recorded on Snapchat, while 9000 photos are being shared through various sites every second. [48]

The aforementioned figures through light over the expansion of internet service in the field of social media and its influence on the society. The increasing trend of using these social media sites might have brought a revolutionary change in the internet world but unfortunately it has turned out into a stage for criminal activities. This fact cannot be ignored that with the emergence of internet and social media networking sites the incidence of various criminals' activities in virtual world has raised in couple of years. The rate at which the social media sites is being used by the perpetrator is a matter of concern, as half of the world is today connected via internet. This situation gets worsened with the overdependence and overuse of internet and social networking sites as the user are more prone to fall prey at the hand of perpetrator. The main idea behind invention of social media was to bring a change in socializing pattern and

---

[48] *Ibid*

2.3 PROS AND CONS OF INTERNET

As every coin has two sides, in the same manner technology has certain benefits and repercussion out of it. The internet has made the world a smaller place where everyone is interconnected with each other in the virtual world. It has also helped people to gather information in search engine and has even become more anonymous in their interactions with others, which has created a certain level of conflict when it comes to privacy of any person. There are many pros and cons of the internet that worth considering at present. Here are some of the main key points.

- **BETTER CONNECTIVITY AND COMMUNICATION:**

In earlier times the method of communication was time consuming and cost oriented. But with the coming up of internet services the we witnessed better connectivity and communication services. The social networking sites has magnified the spectrum of connectivity in every field. Additionally, the social media provided an edge to the communication technology, where one can share their ideas, thoughts and connect with people overseas. It has bridged the cultural differences that existed prior to internet connectivity.

- **BETTER LEARNING:**

Technology has impacted almost every aspect of our life today, and education is no exception to it. Advancement in technology has profoundly changed the whole scenario of education. Today, a massive amount of information in form of-books, audio, images and video are available at one's fingertip within a second on internet. Access to learning opportunities at present time is easy and affordable and all credit goes to internet. Today we have various learning apps such as ByJus, Khans Academy, Unacademy, Brainly, etc. which imparts online education and provides coaching's to the aspirants. One can get education from any part of world just with a click. Education is not just limited to the elites, rather it is now open everyone with the help of internet.

- **ENHANCED JOB OPPORTUNITIES AND BUSINESS EXPANSION:**
  Ever since the commercialization of the internet, the business world has totally evolved from traditional marketing to online shopping the. The dimension of business has expanded far more than ever before. The carrying of business in online mode has strengthen the commercial fields by spreading it to other parts of country. The virtual world has created a huge business boom that no one could have for thought about. In earlier times Along with the business sides of things, people now also have the ability to search and apply for jobs completely through the internet, which has opened up the world job market to many people with valuable skills to offer.[49]

2.3.1 CONS OF INTERNET:

Internet has become an important aspect of our daily life. There is no doubt that it has changed the whole scenario of the world and has brought the world together. But the pace at which the users are becoming over dependent on internet services has marked the challenge of cybercrime, thus affecting the overall growth of an individual and the society as a whole. With all the benefits that lies in its ambit, it certainly brings some disadvantages with it. Some of the major cons of internet are discussed as follow:

INCREASE IN CYBERCRIME:

Looking at the present scenario the internet and the number of its users have grown at a rapid pace. Life without internet seems unimaginable. As people continue to venture into cyberspace and spend most of their time on internet, this conduct has opened the doors for vast opportunities for cybercrime. These offenses are different from traditional crimes such as theft, crimes related to property and fraud, as they comprise of new technology to target their prey in the virtual world. Internet has truly become a universal system of interconnected computer networks that has completely transformed nearly every aspect of human lives. With

---

[49] Impact of Internet Revolution in Business, *available at:* *https://www.managementstudyguide.com* (last visited on June 6, 2021)

the rapid development in internet technology and in cyberspace have truly taken the society to the next level of evolution. The most striking feature of societal evolution is directly connected with the development and use of technology and components associated with it. Internet has served as an essential component featuring the revolutionary development that it brought in our society. Technology has always been prone to be used by the notorious elements of society for their own advantage.[50] Online crime has taken a new route and is simultaneously expanding with the increase use of internet and social networking sites.

Unfortunately, due to the lack of adequate security and ambiguous nature of internet services, there is always a risk revolving around while we access the internet in any form and it becomes impossible to know when the user would become victim of cyber offenders. The current generations increasingly rely on the Internet and advanced technology and this provide an opportunity for the perpetrator to further their criminal operations against the users. Cyber criminals today can easily access the Internet and carry various vicious acts such as cyber harassment, cyber defamation, hack the computer system of the victim, commit online fraud, and even carry out traditional crimes such as trafficking illicit drugs and illegal sex trafficking through the virtual world.[51] Despite having the expansive global recession, improved security, and international efforts to combat the menace of cybercrime, it has rather thrived since last decade by growing at an exponentially speed by doubling year after year. The internet world is frequently evolving its dimension where new criminal threats are emerging as a matter of concern. Various law enforcement agencies and professionals are trying to formulate such an efficient mechanism which work forward to eliminate the grave threat arising out with the changing criminal arena.

DATA BREACH:

Generally speaking, data breach refers to having illegal access to the confidential and personal information of any individual or firm. The concept of data breach is a new concept which emerged out with coming up of online services. Data breach may occur by way of Ransome, Malware, Denial of Service Attack, Phishing etc., in order to get

---

[50] How the Internet Has Changed the Face of Crime, *available at: https://fgcu.digital.flvc.org* (last visited on June 6, 2021)
[51] *Ibid*

confidential credential of the users and commit offence against them. Data breach occurs when the hacker jumps into the computer system of the user and crack their password to gather all relevant information of any individual. The most common type of data breach that occurs in virtual world are credit card breaches, bank details and atm frauds. Data breach has resulted in more

VIRUS ATTACK:

A computer virus is just like a common flu virus which is especially designed to spread from one device to another device and has the ability to replicate itself. Virus attacks is similar in nature like flu, as it cannot reproduce without host in the same manner the viruses need a host to spread from one system to another in form of document or file. Technically speaking a computer virus is a malicious file which is designed to corrupt the whole data stored in computer system such that it spreads from one computer to another. A virus operates as soon as it attaches itself to the files or documents present in any system and disrupt the whole system. A virus has the potential to cause unexpected or damaging effects, such as harming the system software by corrupting or destroying data stored in the system and deleting such data. In the virtual world the computer system is more prone to get effected with the virus attack as we are constantly using internet and social media sites which might get virus hoax inserted in our devices. Viruses can easily get into the system and spread through email and text message attachments, Internet file downloads, and social media scam links. Mobile phones are not exception to it as even it can get infected with mobile viruses which spread through shady apps.[52] Virus hoax companies has expanded in past few decades with the coming up of internet services at an ease.

FAKE INFORMATION:

---

[52] What is a Computer Virus? *available at: https://us.norton.com >internet security* (last visited on June 7, 2021)

At present internet has become a hub of information. It has revolutionized the traditional way of learning and imparting education. Now we do not have spend hours in library looking for the relevant content to enhance our knowledge. Internet has smoothened the way to get information for the students, research scholars and teachers as well. It is a vast platform full of information and content that has made the learning far better than ever before. But unfortunately, this educational domain is being used by some notorious elements to spread fake news for the sake of entertainment or to get popularity in the virtual sphere. There is so much content available online that sometimes it becomes difficult to understand the credibility about such information. Fake news is increasingly becoming a global concern with the increasing trend of using social media sites at a rampant pace. This form of disinformation or irrelevant content is being published online that it has turned out to be violent and grave in nature. There are many instances where fake news has taken away lives of many innocent people. There has been a case in India in 2017 where 7 people were lynched by the local community due to the fake news that circulated on the WhatsApp's claiming them to be child-abductor.[53] This is not the single case, there are many such incidence which takes place within the society but goes unnoticed or unreported due to lack of understanding about the intentions behind such fake news. Today, everyone has access to internet and social media sites, but out of them only few are able to understand the intention behind the content uploaded on internet. Youth and people belonging to marginalized section of the society are more vulnerable to get influenced by such fake news and might get involved in any immoral acts.

INTERNET ADDICTION:

Today Internet addiction has become a major concern for the world as it has affected the mental state of internet users. It is defined as a behavioral addiction in which a person becomes over dependent on use of the Internet, or other online devices to cope up with life stresses. Internet addiction is becoming widely recognized and acknowledged by the world as it is affecting large numbers of people health Taking a glance of the present time it is evident that the internet has increasingly entwined in our lives to such an extent that it has resulted in internet addiction. [54]

---

[53] Indian WhatsApp Lynching, *available at:* https://en.wikipedia.in(last visited on June 7, 2021)
[54] Causes of Internet Addiction -What You Should Know, *available at:* https://www.healthline.com (last visited on June 8, 2021)

The overuse and over dependence of internet and social networking sites has resulted into Internet Addiction Disorder (IAS) in many people who spends most of their time online. Internet addiction is subdivided into 3 mainstreams: online game addiction, online gambling and pornography or online sex addiction. Internet addiction in some cases have been so rave that it led to lose of life. One such example of it was the online game known as "BLUE WHALE" in which the person playing the game was asked to perform some life-threatening acts to get to next level. The level of addiction of this game was so high that many people committed suicide. The "Blue Whale challenge" was reported to be an online "suicide game" where the main target was aimed at teenagers which set 50 tasks over 50 days. It allegedly took many innocent lives. Many said it to be a well-planned cold blood murder, where the game played with the minds of youth and forcing them to commit suicide.[55] It was the most horrific and traumatizing thing that shook whole world.

Moreover, increasing addiction to mobile phones and social media has contributed a lot towards internet addiction. The Internet Addiction Disorder is prevalent in youths and between the age group ranging from mid 30s to late 50s. The impact of internet addiction seems passive in nature as it is yet to be recognized as a disease at national level, but the repercussion of its addiction is far beyond one's imagination. It may lead to withdrawal symptoms, anxiety, mood swings, depression and in extreme cases it might lead to suicide by the victim. Internet addiction has even recognized as an important factor that has contributed the most in rapid increase in cybercrime cases worldwide.

2.4 CYBER CRIME: A HISTORICAL ACCOUNT

Crime has been a part of the human civilization since time immemorial. It has been evolving its nature with the passage of time. In earlier times, the act which was recognized as criminal act was the one which was committed against the state. Gradually as the time passed and human civilization got revolutionized, it gave importance to human rights and imposed a moral duty on every individual to respect the basic fundamental rights of every individual and the one who violates it was punished. Therefore, for the first time any malicious act committed against an individual was considered as crime. The definition of crime is not constant, rather it has been changing as the nature of crime evolved. In present time, the definition of crime has expanded its dimension to the virtual world. Nowadays, crimes are not

---

[55] Blue Whale Challenge, *available at:* https://www.wikipedia.in (last visited on June 8, 2021)

just committed in traditional ways such as crime against property, murder or fraud, but it has found new scope in virtual world. The cyberspace is the new room for all kinds of criminal acts today. Cybercrime too got evolved with the new technology. Earlier cybercrimes were committed through telecommunication but later on with the invention of internet networking the cyber offence shifted from telecommunication mode to online mode. To understand the emergence and evolution of cyber crime in cyber world it's important to know the historical account of it.

CYBERCRIME IN 80s:

Technically, the first ever reported cyberattack happened in France in 1834 prior to invention of internet. It was an era where people used to communicate with others through telegraph system. The perpetrators attacked the French Telegraph system and stole away all relevant information of financial market. From that time period the world has witnessed an exponential growth in cybercrime cases, marked by an interesting history of usage of various tactics, techniques, and procedures committed to get malicious gain out of it.[56]

1940s: THE TIME BEFORE CYBERCRIME

It was a time when the computer was invented. It was the greatest invention of mankind, which transformed the whole communication system. But at that time computer system was not available for the use of public, it was limited to carry out experiments and for military purposes only. Cybercrime was also limited only because it was quite tricky to target those big computers, therefore only less opportunity was there for the perpetrators to carry their malicious acts. It was time when criminals were active on telephonic medium and computer was used only by few people. Interestingly it was in 1949 that the theory related to virus attack on computer system was propounded by the experts. The virus attacks and concept of cyber security got momentum from this time period as it was the only two most prominent concept underlying the theory of crime.[57]

---

[56] The Fascinating Decade in Cybercrime :2010-2020, *available at: https://arcticwolf.com* (last visited on June 10, 2021)
[57] *Ibid*

1950: THE TIME PERIOD FOR PHONE PHREAKERS:

Hacking of system is not new, it dates back to the time period when hacking was done through telephones. The concept of "phone-phreaking "came into light in the late1950s. The concept of phone -phreaking caught the attention of the telecommunication companies when the cases of call -dropping started reporting. Basically, the hackers who were good at working with phones used to hijack those protocols which helped the telecom engineers to work on network that made free calls. Phone hacking eventually ended up in 1980 with the coming up of internet services.

1960s: COMPUTER RELATED CRIMES:

In early period of 1960s, the access to computer system was still limited. As the computers at that time were large in size and it required a room that had controlled temperature. Due to the inbuilt quality and size issue of the older computer, the cases of cybercrime were far too less. But in late 60s the computer manufacturing industry brought changes in the system by manufacturing compact size computer, so that its easy to purchase and be used by everyone. This change in the scientific sphere was a stepping stone towards a new generation. It was time when computer sabotage has gained prominence in the virtual world.

1970s: BIRTH OF COMPUTER SECURITY

With the passage the use of computer devices was increasing simultaneously thus enhancing the technology. While the scientist was working over enhancing the communication service through computers, the concern over breach of data was raised. Keeping this in mind the cyber security was developed and it started working in 1972 with the research project on ARPANET.

The vulnerabilities of cybercrime increased as the emerging technologies became more open to all and now more organizations were starting telecommunication services to create network. Each new element of technology opened a gateway entry for the hackers and it was important to safeguard the data saved in computers, therefore, concept of cyber security was promulgated at international forum.

As reliance on computers increased and networking area grew, the government got a clear picture that its necessary to have cyber security to avoid any unauthorized access to data. By 1972-1974 the global market witnessed an increase in discussion about computer security.[58] All the research academy and the defense body recognized the importance of computer security to avoid any future menace. Even today cyber security has been a hot topic of millennium due to the ever increase in cybercrimes, thus, it becomes duty for the national and international bodies to priorities the need for better cyber security to avoid cybercrimes.

1980s EMERGENCE OF INTERNET FROM ARPANET

Internet services was the outcome of establishment of ARPANET by the U.S government at the time of cold war. The U.S government established ARPANET to enhance their communication network in case the Soviet Union attacked the U.S defense coops. At its initial stage ARPANET was a Wide Area Network which worked as a program to link many Universities and research centers to carry their field work easily and was first to use the concept of packet switching and, therefore was a landmark stone at the beginning of what we consider the Internet world today. ARPANET was created with an aim to provide a better service program that made easier for people to access computers, and to have a more effective communication method for the military officials. Later on, in late 80s it was no longer an experimental base service, rather the communication facilities got enhanced and was utilized by the commerce sector at a large extent. Even today, ARPANET is considered as the backbone of internet.[59]

It was with the advent of ARPANET that the internet service was developed and used by the public at large. Internet was gaining importance day by day and became a part of life of every user.

1990s THE WORLD GOES ONLINE:

---

[58] The History of Cyber Crime and Cyber Security ,1940-2020, *available at:* https://cybersecurityventure.com (last visited on June 10, 2021)
[59] *Ibid 31*

In early 1990s the internet services went viral and was made available to public. Those who had computer system were able to access the internet services and enjoy its benefit. Gradually every home had computer system and the demand of internet service was also rising. While the world was going online, the predominance of virus attacks was getting quite frequent. By the year 1996, there were rampant increase in virus attacks as many viruses used new techniques and methods to corrupt the computer data. This posed a threat to the company's manufacturing computers and to the antivirus vendors who were working over virus attacks.[60]

By early 90s, the number of new viruses and malware exploded. Where earlier the number of virus attacks was limited to tens and thousands, now the number of virus relatively increased to millions. By mid 90s the experts showed their concern over need of cybersecurity and proposed that idea of mass-production of antivirus to protect the public data.

2000: THE ERA OF SOCIAL MEDIA

Internet was becoming an important part of our lifestyle steadily. But its usage accelerated at a rapid pace with the invention of social networking sites. It completely changed the whole scenario of the communication mode. At that time "Orkut" was the most frequent used social networking site operated by Google, which was designed in such way which helped its users to meet new and old friends via their Orkut account and cherish their existing relationship with friends. Over the years Orkut gained popularity and was the favorite social networking site for the youth. But later on, this platform was removed from internet and a new social media platform was developed which completely changed the internet world and was known as "FACEBOOK". Facebook emerged as the world's largest social media platform online playing a significant role in daily lives of its users. From past few years its daily active user base has grown year-over-year thus, bringing the world together on one platform. According to a survey there are 1.73 billion daily users of Facebook and this number increases at 11% every year. It has become a global platform with over 2.6 million monthly active users worldwide.[61]

---

[60] A Brief History of Cybercrime -Florida Tech Online, available *at:* *https://www.floridatechonline.com* *(last visited on June 11, 2021)*
[61] How Many People Uses Facebook in 2021, *available at: https://backlinko.com >Blog* (last visited on June 11, 2021)

The social media platform has a great influence over its user, as the number of daily active users is exponentially increasing. In addition to Facebook there are other social media platform as well which has dramatically changed the whole world. Facebook being the largest used social media platform is followed by You Tube with over 260 million users. There are other apps such as WhatsApp, Messenger, Instagram, Twitter, WeChat, Telegram etc., with 56.89% active users.[62]

These social media sites have diversified the human civilization by breaking all the cultural and geographical barriers. With the social media we are now heading towards a world where states are Net-Connected. In between, with an ominous development of social engaging platforms the misuse of social media has also cropped up.[63]

A serious problem of cyber offences has emerged in the virtual world and the fact cannot be ignored that social media has invited all sorts of criminal activities to take place in cyber space. These social media sites have changed the nature and mode in which crime is instituted against an individual or any firm. With the trend of posting a detailed account of day-to-day activities on social media sites provides an opportunity to the perpetrators to commit crime against the users. There have been reported cases of bullying, defamation, publishing of obscene content online, fraud, cheating and infringement of privacy of the users.

The threat of online crime is not limited to individual only, but it even hinders with the social order. There is an obstacle while accessing these sites as the misinformation which it feeds to its users are fake and affect their decision-making capability. This fake information might trigger anger or agitation among the user against any person or particular society thus, resulting into hate crimes. Mob lynching, hate crimes, bullying and blackmailing are at rise due to the fake information served on the social media platform. This not only affects the mental state of the victim but also create haphazard in the social order. By such crimes the social order faces challenges as anonymity overshadow the wrongdoer identity and making difficult for the law agencies to punish such person.

Social media sites have overpowered the perpetrators to commit crime in the virtual world at an ease. With million of users having access to these social networking sites makes it easy to hunt for the targeted victim without being caught. Cybercrimes are at surge with the coming

---

[62] *Ibid*
[63] Vidya Sagar," Social Media-A Boon and A Bane ", Times of India, April 25,2019

of social media sites, as the individual lack the knowledge to understand the criminal intent in the virtual world. Therefore, need to regulate these social media apps becomes necessary to maintain social order and safeguard the interest of its users.

2010: THE 10TH GENERATION WORLD

The 10th generation in the tech world has changed the overall framework of internet around the globe. The 10th generation is marked with the beginning of the time where whole world goes tech savvy. The invention of smartphones, smartwatches and tablet has expanded the use of internet to next level. Smartphones has magnificently turned the internet into a blessing for mankind. But as the technology advanced it got converted into curse with the crime taking place in the virtual world. It completely changed the whole scenario of commission of crime. The ease of hi-tech technology might have served a good mean for human but on the other side the grave breaches of public interest is also at large. The gravity of crime that is committed in the virtual world is haunting and terrifying in nature. Virus attack and data breach is the common cause of cybercrime of the 10th generation. As the technology is advancing, the crime is finding loopholes in it to penetrate in the society by any means. In past few years from 2010-2019 the cyber crime has found new ways to target the victim and has gained momentum just short span of time period. Although there are various statutes to regulate the conduct of perpetrators but we need more advanced method to combat the ever-growing menace of cyber crime in the real world.[64]

2.5 UBIQUITY OF CYBER CRIME

Cybercrime or computer related crimes are classified into new form of crimes which are committed in virtual space. Unlike traditional crimes, these crimes are more complex and wittier in nature. Crime has been there in society since ages and has gradually transformed itself with passage of time. Where earlier it was limited to certain place or territory, today it can be carried out from any part of the world with the help of internet service. Presently, crime has evolved with technology and has a greater edge than ever before. As the

---

[64] *Ibid 48*

Information Technology (IT)sector developed so did the cybercrime. It became more sophisticated, more lucrative, complex and profitable in comparison to the traditional way of committing crime. It became a global phenomenon within a short span. To understand the changing dimension of cybercrime it is important to understand how it differs from traditional crimes.

2.5.1 DIFFERENCE BETWEEN TRADITIONAL CRIMES AND CYBERCRIME

In the simplest term's cybercrime is describ3ed as a criminal act committed by taking the aid of technology and the internet. In order to understand the concept of cybercrime it is important that we know the difference between the traditional crime and computer related crime. In the case of cyber-crimes, it is not committed in the real world and thus, it is relatively hard to locate the culprit, distinguish between the real and fake culprit and get caught of him.

The biggest and the most obvious difference between the two above mentioned head is that it is tough to get proof of offence in cyber offences than the traditional one. In traditional crimes the culprit often ends up leaving some or the other traceable evidence of crime, such as finger prints, the weapon used or any other confirmation about himself. Contrary to it, in virtual space it is easy to commit crime and there is no chance of being caught as no proof is left behind by cyber criminals. They carry out the malicious act with sophistication and are professionals who have knowledge about the IT and are well acquainted with new technology. [65]

When it comes to examination of culprits, it becomes difficult to locate the offenders, as they commit offences from different location and this tend to make cybercrime more dangerous for society then the traditional crime. Cybercrime is carried out with the aid of internet and it helps the culprit to carry even some traditional crimes such as defamation, terrorism, bulling, stalking, assault etc.

---

[65] *Supra 2 178*

Another significant difference between the two is that its really difficult to investigate cybercrime and find out the real offender, as they use distorted names and identity to constitute various offences. Whereas in traditional crimes the investigation and examination of the culprit takes less time and the collection of evidence is easy as the culprit leaves behind hints on spot. For example, the customary offenders leave behind evidences such as: fingerprints, identity card, or other physical confirmation which ultimately help to find the offender.

Over the years the habitual offenders are changing their ideal way of carrying out criminal acts with the help of new technology equipment. Cyber criminals are offer put in the category of habitual offender as they are more sophisticated, well- experienced and are professionals. There is a shift in the way traditional crime takes place. At present most of the traditional crimes are constituted via online mode such as fraud, money laundering, online gambling, theft etc. Cyber crime has been evolving itself from time to time as according to the profit gained out of it. Cybercrimes are more profitable and flexible to commit and this has changed the status of cybercrime to transnational or syndicated crimes.

2.5.2 SYNDICATED CYBERCRIME

Over the years, world have witnessed a drastic change in our social setup. As the world went online the cultural difference which existed earlier in our society got replaced with mutual understanding and establishing a platform where ideas from different cultures are exchanged and adopted worldwide. Information Technology bridged the gap that existed earlier between various diversified cultures. On one hand it brought the world together but on the other side it gave birth to cybercrimes.

Internet services and social media platform has accelerated the cybercrimes and it has resulted in syndicated cybercrime. In simplest term syndicated crimes are the criminal acts which are performed by a group with common intention. They usually occur in order to carry out a well-executed criminal plan and commit the same with consensus of all. At present, the cybercrime has turned into more syndicated form of crime, committed to get monetary profit out of it. These syndicated cyber crimes are being carried out on a large scale and the most profound one is as follow:

2.5.3 ONLINE DRUG TRAFFICKING:

The abuse and trafficking of narcotic and psychotropic drugs has existed in our society from a longer period of time and has been a matter of concern for the states. But in recent years with the rise in new technology, especially with overdependence on internet has aggravated this issue. Illegal distribution of drugs over internet has increased over time and has affected many countries. The domestic pharmaceutical companies have turned to internet services to expand their business and this has provided a great opportunity for the domestic abuser to get drugs online. The dispensing of pharmaceutical drugs over internet has facilitates the trafficking of drugs in an easy manner. The internet provides a platform which is accessible and virtually anonymous for the buyer as well as seller as they share no personal information.[66]

The trend of online pharmaceutical business has seen a sudden rise in illegal drug trafficking. As most of the sites are not recognized they sell the drugs without any prescriptions. While some companies provide service of having a telephonic consultation with the physician and they prescribe particular medicine to the patient. The vulnerabilities of online drug trafficking increases in such cases as the physician might be the drug peddler who acts as a doctor to sell illegal drugs by legal method.[67]This forms a base for syndicated online cybercrime, where internet is being used as a medium to carry out illicit drug trafficking in virtual space. These culprits sell the contrabands through internet as it is easy and anonymity in the cyber space helps them to escape any legal prosecution. Moreover, selling illicit drugs online is more profitable and flexible than selling on streets.

Online drug trafficking has seriously posed a challenge for the law enforcement agencies. The organized criminal groups misuse the internet services to sell the drugs online and make it available to the buyer without any hinderances. On an average drug make up to two thirds of all kind of cyber offences carried on the dark web. [68]

The most vulnerable group which indulges in the aforementioned crimes are the youth. Due to easy access of internet services the problem of drug trafficking among youth is quite prominent. With no regulation over these pharmaceutical firms, even children can obtain any pharmaceutical substance after entering accurate information about their age and ailments.

---

[66] Drugs in Cyberspace: Understanding and Investigation, *available at: http://www.cicad.oas.org* > Farma-doc (last visited on June 12, 2021)
[67] *Ibid*
[68] Drug trafficking dominates the darknet, *available at : https://www.dw.com* (last visited on June 11, 2021)

According to a survey conducted in 2005, it was revealed that 19% of teens have abused the prescribed drugs in their lifetime.[69] Thus, with the easy access to internet services it is being witnessed worldwide that the organized criminal groups selling the drugs online and are making great profit out of it. This has been a major concern for all the nations as it poses threat to the national security and challenges the legal framework of nation state.

2.5.4 ONLINE HUMAN TRAFFICKING AND SEXUAL EXPLOITATION

Generally human trafficking is referred as trafficking in persons. It is a form of modern-day slavery which involves transportation of individual by illegal means, by force for the purpose of labor, sexual exploitation or any other activity which yields monetary benefit. Human trafficking is a global problem affecting people of all ages. On an average approximately 1,000,000 people are trafficked each year globally.[70]

On an average nearly three quarters of victims of human trafficking includes women and girls and three out of four of these are particularly trafficked for sexual exploitation only. Human trafficking is referred as a crime against humanity and has been a matter of concern for every nation. The major factor which has contributed to increase in human trafficking at present is marked by internet services and social media sites. The organized criminal groups are misusing this platform of information to commit crime against humanity and carry out online trafficking of humans.

Today internet is becoming a huge platform where the perpetrators use internet as a medium to sell and buy women and children and push them into a world where they are sexually exploited. Although the trafficking in women and children especially for sexual exploitation is not a new phenomenon, as it is followed from the very earlier times. The trade of female bodies for sex has been there in the society from the beginning of patriarchy. However, with the rise of technology and the growth of online connectivity, the trafficking women and girls into commercial sex industry has become smoother and safer for the traffickers globally.[71]

---

[69] *Ibid*
[70] Human Trafficking |Definition, Tactics, Statistics, Type, available at: *www.britanica.com* (Last visited on June 11, 2021)
[71] Trafficked Women and Girls Sold Online, *available at: https://www.youngfeminist.eu* (last visited on June 11,

The internet is becoming a hub for such cybercrimes against human, as online trafficking takes place in form of pornography, shared video of abuse of women etc.

Online sexual exploitation has increased many folds. Women and children may be sold through live video calls. Trafficked women and children are advertised and sold online through adult sites or through general advertising platforms. It is to no surprise that internet has made women and girls more vulnerable to fall prey at the hands of traffickers and it has been found that a whole range of video and picture of exploited women or girls are available at online sites in form of pornography.[72]

Among all social media is the key to all sorts of sexual offences that takes place in virtual world. It has made the women section of society more vulnerable to become victim to this modernized event of sex trafficking. Social media has made it easy for the traffickers to target the women and girls easily in large number and commit cybercrime against them. The Internet and social media sites have relatively made it easy for the syndicated criminals to sell and buy the women online. Internet and social media serve an easy method to force women and girls to indulge in sexual activities and even sell them to the buyers at higher cost. Thus, the traffickers make huge profit out of selling women and girls via online as its affordable and safer place.

2.6 INTERNET AS A TOOL FOR CYBER WARFARE

Throughout the history, mankind has waged war against each other to attain supremacy among all nations and further seek their agenda of becoming world power. World have witnessed blood shedding wars ranging from sword battles of past to nuclear bomb of World War, the game of power has been shifting as the technology got advanced and multifarious. As the times passed by, there was a huge development in defense mechanism with the invention of o armored vehicles, aircraft, ships and the use of electronics and telecommunications. This growth in defense sector expanded the scope of battle and introduced far mor better innovative ideas to gain supremacy over the opponent nation. As the

2021)

[72] Ibid

technology Advancement took place in the field of defense, a race triggered among the nation to attain the supremacy and be a world power. [73]

A great deal of fact is that world has already faced the brunt of World War and other warfare situations, so in order to avoid any war in future every nation state came together to sign the Peace Treaty and avoid any such grave breached of humanity further. Various Treaties and Conventions were signed by most of the nation party who were member of United Nations (UN). But irrespective of that we have seen many inter-state wars taking place around globe, be it Indo-Pak, America- Mexico or the recent one Israel-Palestine war and many more. But certainly, the use of nuclear weapons or any such dangerous equipment's during war are still avoided. But the biggest threat which has been predicted to define many future international wars and clashes are related with "CYBERWARFARE".

Cyberwarfare is defined as a network-based attack on nations, citizens, and governments carried through computer system via online mode. Cyber space is considered as the future zone for war in upcoming time. Cyber warfare involves the use of online technology to attack cybersecurity system of any country, especially for military purpose, financial gain or cyber-espionage. As the internet gained importance in the sphere of crimes that took place in the cyber space, it even empowered the extremist to conduct cyberwarfare against any nation. Such an attack could be initiated by some terrorist group, or hacker or some extremist who harm the nations security to spread their propaganda or to get pecuniary benefit out of it.[74]

At present Cyberwarfare is the most challenging crime for the states to identify as it leaves no room for speculations. It can take place by hacking the nations computer system and gather all relevant information about the national policy through computer viruses, data breach, malware and denial-of service attacks. It could be used by one nation against other nation to threaten the peace and security of the targeted nation, cause economic loss to them and leads to collapse of nation. With easy availability of internet across the globe, chances of cyberwarfare have also grown and it poses a threat for the developed as well as developing nations to secure their data in order to protect their nation from cyber attack and protect the citizens from such war kind situation in future.

---

[73] What is Cyberwarfare? - Search security, available at: *https://searchsecurity.techtarget.com* (last visited on June 13, 2021)
[74] *Ibid*

2.7 CHRONOLOGY OF REGULATIONS RELATING CYBER CRIME

With the development of computer system and invention of internet services, the criminal offences related to its use had also increased. While the cyberspace has provided an opportunity for the world to come together on one platform and remove all social disparities that existed prior to coming up of IT sector. But cyberspace has also created a bunch of new opportunities for the perpetrators to use it as a medium for commission of crime. It has opened door for criminal activities to further carry global attacks on the basic foundation of sovereign states and other grave cybercrimes.

The threat of cyber-attack is becoming a common phenomenon day by day. Today the global cyberattacks are not limited to be constituted against an individual or any business firm rather it has extended its root far beyond our imagination and may even constitute a threat to international peace and security. With the world going online mankind is under threat of cybercrimes every second they access the internet services and therefore, need for a global framework to promote peace, security and justice arises. To protect the interest of every individual and preserve the sovereignty of state, a global framework on cybersecurity and cybercrime is necessary to combat the menace and threat that is there in cyberspace, and invite such measures that may reduce the prevailing risk of cybercrime.

To preserve the integrity of nations, special strategies need to be adopted for a common understanding on cybersecurity and cybercrime. Every nation needs to come together and frame such policies that curb the growing menace of cyber-attacks and preserve economic development of every nation state. A global cybersecurity framework may reduce risks factor and threats in cyberspace, and lay down provisions for essential architecture in national and international solutions.

As the world showed concern over ever growing problem of cybercrime various dialogues were exchanged between the nations to adopt such policies to set standard for crime committed in cyber space and provide a better cybersecurity. Regional and bilateral agreements were not be sufficient in upholding such sensitive issue, thus various recommendations were made, conventions and treaties were signed to stop cybercrime to some extent. International law is necessary to make the global society able to respond to cyberattacks and cybercrimes.[75]

2.7.1 COUNCIL OF EUROPE:

The first ever international initiative that was taken while keeping in mind the concerned problem of rise in cybercrime in Europe was the Council of Europe Conference on Criminological Aspects of Economic Crime in Strasbourg in 1976. The council addressed to the various aspect of cyber offences and the threat that it posed to national security and several categories of computer crime were introduced by the council to mark a clear distinction between traditional crime and cybercrime.[76]

2.7.2 THE INTERPOL

The International Criminal Police Organization which is commonly known by the name as INTERPOL. INTERPOL is an international organization that smoothen the relationship among the police worldwide and control crime. It is the world largest police organization with 194-member state and headquarter located in Lyon.[77]

INTERPOL established procedure for investigative support, expertise, and training to law enforcement worldwide, which focus on three most prominent areas of transnational crime: terrorism, cybercrime, and organized crime. Its principal mandate covers all those crimes which are committed against humanity and includes child pornography, drug trafficking, white-collar crimes, sexual exploitation of women and girls, cyber terrorism, corruption and crime against intellectual property.

Interpol was the first international organization addressing computer crime and penal legislation at a Conference in Paris in 1979. It focused on the steady growth of cybercrime and focused on forming more International Organization to combat the cybercrime. It proposed the idea of modifying the present cybersecurity system in order to avoid data breach.

---

[75] The History of Global Harmonization Cybercrime Legislation, available at: *https://cybercrimelaw.net* (last visited on June 13, 2021)
[76] *Ibid*
[77] Interpol, available *at*: *https://wikipedia.in* (last visited on June 13, 2021)

2.7.3 INTERNATIONAL TELECOMMUNICATION UNION (ITU) IN GENEVA

ITU is active Institution of United Nation which has reached over the harmonization of global cybersecurity and cybercrime legislation at Geneva in May 2007, the Secretary-General of the ITU proposed a Global Cybersecurity Agenda (GCA) for a framework where the international response over the growing challenges to cybersecurity was discussed. GCA in a broader sense is the framework for proposing effective solutions to enhance confidentiality and security in the information society, under the umbrella of cyber security. ITU in Geneva proposes the developing nations to come together to follow the protocol on cyber security and combating cybercrime.[78]

2.7.4 THE BUDAPEST CONVENTION ON CYBERCRIME

The Convention on Cybercrime, also known as the Budapest Convention on Cybercrime or the Budapest Convention. It is the first ever international treaty which seeks to address the computer related crimes and regulate the cyber laws by harmonizing national laws on computer related crimes, improve investigation techniques, rely importance on e-evidence and harmonize corporation among nations.[79]

The Budapest Convention lays down certain provisions which provides for the criminalization of conduct which ranges from illegal access, data and systems interference to computer-related fraud and child pornography, lays procedural law tools to make further investigation of cybercrime and securing of e-evidence in relation to any crime more effectively, and define the role of international police and need for judicial cooperation on cybercrime and e-evidence.[80]

At present cybercrime concerns every person, no one can escape from it – be it any company, authority or any public institution. The reality is that the origin as well as the target of the criminal act can be located virtually everywhere around the globe and we never know when

---

[78] *Ibid* 64
[79] The Budapest Convention and General Data Protection Regulation, available at: *https://link.springer.com >article* (last visited on June 14, 2021)
[80] *Ibid*

the culprits would attack the users. Currently, cybercrime has set a new challenge for lawmakers in their efforts to protect society against this new sort of crime.

Due to our overdependence on use of internet might have created conveniences for the public to enjoy but at the same time it opens countless doors for hackers to gain unauthorized access to devices, networks and valuable data, all of which is generally being abused for criminal acts. The Budapest Convention on Cybercrime plays a crucial role in combating the menace of cybercrime by setting out some important principle based on criminal law standards and important procedural rules while dealing with cybercrime cases. The article enshrined in the Budapest convention clearly define the acts which constitute as crime and relevant punishment for the offender.

In addition to it, the General Data Protection Regulation (GDPR) has taken the lead for the appropriate handling of data, and lays down significant procedure to improve the data security and enhanced mechanism dealing with cybercrime.[81]

2.7.5 EMERGING TREND OF CYBER FORENSIC

Cyber space is a physical space which only exists in the cyber world and has nothing to do with the real world. Cyber-attacks and cyber abuse usually take place in the cyberspace itself. Cyberspace provide protection to the culprits and they often use this as an opportunity to commit cybercrime. Due to the flexible nature of cyber space the perpetrators get an easy hand to escape the prosecution as no evidence is available against them. This situation posed a serious threat for the law-making agencies to combat the menace of cybercrime. In order to deal with such situation, the invention of Computer Forensic or Cyber Forensic took place.

In literal sense cyber forensic is the tool which is used in investigation process to gather and preserve the evidence which are collected from a particular computer device through which crime was instituted and such evidence are preserved in such manner to be presented before court of law.

The main postulate of computer forensics is to carry out a well-structured or well planned a investigation and maintain a record of documented chain of evidence to find out the nature of

---

[81] General Data Protection Regulation, available at: *https://en.wikipedia.com* (last visited on June 14, 2021)

crime that was committed through such computing device and to gather the identity of the culprit.

Computer forensics is generally referred to as computer forensic science which is developed for data recovery with legal compliance guidelines to make the information as admissible while the matter is in legal proceedings. [82] It makes the legal proceedings more flexible, easy and the evidence presented are reliable and saves the time of the court as well.

The main reason for adopting this scientific investigation was that in the civil and criminal justice system, computer forensics helps in ensuring the integrity of digital evidence presented in court cases. As computers and other data-collecting devices are being used more frequently used in every aspect of life the cybercrimes also increased, thereby it was important to have a scientific approach to collect digital evidence to further the investigation and solve cybercrimes.[83]

The average person never sees much of the information modern devices collect. For instance, the computers in cars continually collect information on when a driver brakes, shifts and changes speed without the driver being aware. However, this information can prove critical in solving a legal matter or a crime, and computer forensics often plays a role in identifying and preserving that information. The digital evidence has proven to be of great importance for solving crimes committed in cyberspace as well as in tracing the traditional criminals who commit crime in real world. Thus, the fact cannot be ignored that cyber forensic is the digital wellbeing which can help in curbing the cybercrime worldwide.

2.8 CYBER CRIME IN CONTEMPORARY TIME

The usage of internet and social media services has turned the world into a global village. At present the use of internet and social media are at rise. From online shopping, to work from home or from imparting education, everything is online. In the contemporary time period, the world has seen a great influence of internet in the society. The shift that has occurred in our

---

[82] What is Computer Forensic? (Cyber Forensic), *available at:* https://www.searchsecurity.techtarget.com (last visited on June 14, 2021)
[83] *Ibid*

normal life with the coming up of digitalization has opened doors for the perpetrators to invade in the personal sphere of an individual and victimize them for their own interest.

As on today, where day to day work is being carried online, be it work from home, business transactions, educational training, bill payments etc. People are spending hours and hours sitting in front of computer system or clinging onto their mobile to access internet services. With the exposure to internet and unlimited things available online has made human more chronical to become an internet addict. People who spend most of their time online surfing net or social media sites are more prone to have symptoms of depression, anxiety disorder, experience withdrawal symptoms and even led to obesity in youths. The story doesn't end here, with our over dependence on internet and spending most of the time on social media poses a threat of cybercrime.

By just taking a look over the increased number of cybercrime cases in few years, have raised the concern about the ever-lasting impact that it holds on the victim. The cyber criminals are not a common person, but are well trained and sophisticated professionals, who are well versed with new technology. These criminals look forward an opportunity to target the individual person by getting illegal access to their devices and gather all information about them. After stealing all the relevant credential about the targeted person, they are blackmailed, harassed and sometimes forced into criminal intimidation. These offences are not committed by a single person, rather it has now turned into a syndicated offence and number or people work in group to carry cyber offences.

Looking at the historical evolution of internet and cybercrime, one can conclude that, cyber offences are becoming more transnational in nature and are getting graver day by day and has penetrated its root deep into our system, thus disrupting the moral aspect of society. Unlike earlier, where crimes were committed against the business firms or state in order to get financial profit, is now heading towards targeting women and young children of tender age. The changing spectrum of cybercrime has endured enormous risk to life of women who being targeted by the cyber criminals. Human trafficking and drug trafficking are getting more intense with the technological advancement. Online platform has made it easy for the offender from all parts of the world to come together on one stage and carry transnational crimes.

In contemporary era the scope of crimes has significantly seen a change in the manner it is carried out. Internet has turned into a crime space where one can easily invade into personal life of the user through various social media sites and infringe their basic rights. Cyberspace is turning more or less into a spiderweb where one easily gets trapped and has no way to escape. It invites people around the globe to inter-change their thoughts and usually liker-minded criminals tend to abet the commission of crime and generates benefit out of it. This challenges the legal framework of every nation and weakens the security of nation. Various malware and virus attacks on the security system of national security raise doubt over the efficacy of legal statues which are construed to protect the citizens from any violence.

Cyber terrorism and cyber warfare pose a great risk on overall inter-state relationship of nations around the globe. Therefore, it is a high time for the nation states to come together and sign treaties which especially are formulated to curb the threat of cyber-attacks which has caused unrest in our society. To avoid any future war between world power arising due to cyberwarfare, it is necessary to regulate internet services and have strong security system which cannot be easily destroyed and then only the aim of crime free society can be achieved

LEGAL PROVISIONS ON CYBER CRIME AGAINST WOMEN

CHAPTER 3

3.1 CYBER CRIME AND LAW

Information Technology has brought a revolutionary change in our daily life. One of the biggest contributions made by IT sector to the mankind was inventing Internet Service. Today the internet has covered vast dimension of living sphere and has become an important aspect of everybody's daily life. Be it form the very basic daily needs shopping to communication with friends it has completely taken over the world. Its usage is not just limited to individual only, rather companies have also opted to continue their operations through the web which has simultaneously resulted in rise of e-commerce. The scope of internet does not end here, with the idea of going digital many government operations are also taking place online with rise of e-finance in couple of years. Internet has made life easy and comfortable.

Looking at the present scenario, it can be asserted that violence against women is rising at an alarming rate. Violence against women (VAW) which is peculiarly known as gender-based violence and sexual and gender-based violence (SGBV) are considered those acts which are violent in nature and exclusively committed against women or girls. These offences are gender- based and the offender usually target the vulnerable section of society especially women and girls in any forms. The VAW has a vast history, it is as old as the society itself and the intensity of such violence vary from time to time between societies. Since ancient period, women have always been subjected to all sorts of violence in comparison to the male section of society. The reason behind such violence in literal sense generally arises from the sense of entitlement, male predominance in the society, superiority complex, or the socio-cultural aspect of patriarchal setup.

The notion that "women is slave to men and not an equal of men" is still practiced in our society today and they are subjected to violence and cruelty. Violence against women can fit into several broad categories and it includes sexual offences as rape, sexual harassment, domestic violence, acid attacks, reproductive coercion, female infanticide, prenatal sex selection, obstetric violence, as well as there are some customary or traditional practices such as honor killings, dowry violence, female genital mutilation and forced marriage by abduction. Other

3.2 IMPORTANCE OF CYBER LAWS

In today's techno-savvy environment, the world is getting more advanced and digitally sophisticated. This has widened the scope of cybercrime as well. Initially internet was developed as a research tool and information gathering source. With the passage of time internet became more of what transactional in nature with coming up of e- commerce, e-business, e-governance etc. As the world went for digitalization, the area for cybercrime also widened up. In order to deal with this situation there arises a need to have concrete legal structure to combat cybercrime. All legal issues related to internet crime are dealt with through cyber laws. As the instances of online offences arises, need for cyber laws and their application has also gathered great momentum at present.[84]

In today's highly digitalized world, every aspect of life is regulated by cyber law. For example:

- Most of the transactions are being carried out in online which are regulated by cyber laws.
- With the emergence of internet all the companies are going for e-commerce and store their data in electronic form.
- Government forms of tax payment, company forms and other forms are filled online.
- Credit card and debit card usage is also bound by some regulations.

---

[84] Cyber law: A Comprehensive Guide for 2021, *available at: https://www.jigsawacademy.com* (last visited on June 14, 20210

The importance of cyber laws is not just limited to regulate the transaction taking place online. It even helps in solving crimes that does not takes place in cyber space. For instance, any conventional crime that take place in physical world, evidence in such case such as data or identity stored in phone or computer devices can be gathered where crime against human takes place. It even aid in locating offenders of economic offences such as tax evasion, counterfeiting currency etc.[85]

Cybercrime cases such as online banking frauds, online share trading fraud, code theft, credit card fraud, tax evasion, virus attacks, cyber sabotage, phishing attacks, email hijacking, denial of service, hacking, pornography, online fraud, electronic money laundering etc. are becoming common every day. Digitalization has made the cyber space a vulnerable space to carry their business or their official work as threat of cybercrime is always there. Apart from these perpetrators use the cyber space to carry wrong doing against an individual for their vengeance. Crime based on gender are very prominent in virtual world and thus it becomes crucial for the law agency to form such laws which irradicate the crimes which have penetrated deep into our society.

At a broader aspect technology per se is never a disputed issue until and unless it cost the life of someone. The prevailing atmosphere of cybercrime has forced the government to take the issue in its ambit. The cyber revolution holds the promise of quickly reaching the masses in comparison to the earlier technologies, but this revolutionary change had even brought some challenges with it which had a trickle-down effect on social order.

While keeping in mind all the repercussion that the internet usage has, its mandatory to have cyber laws which deals with particular case involving computer related offences. Just like any other laws, Cyber law consists of rules and regulations that direct how the internet and computer system should be used by the people and the companies. Unlike any other law, cyber law protects the interest of people and save them from being trapped in cybercrime. Although it's quite impossible for any legal system to eliminate crime in any form from society, but still the laws hold some weightage when it comes to addressing the concern issue of crime. Similarly, cybercrime cannot be fully eliminated but with the effective laws it can be regulated. The importance of Cyber law can be understood by the following points:[86]

- It keeps a check over all actions that takes place in Cyberspace

---

[85] *Ibid*
[86] *Ibid 74*

- It ensures safe and protected online transactions
- Cyber law empowers the Cyber Law Officials to keep a vigilant check over illegal activities taking place online
- It ensures data security of all individuals, business firms and government organization
- It helps in restoring the relevant data which possesses legal value
- Helps in curbing the cybercrime menace
- Protects the privacy right of every individual
- Sets out provisional laws while dealing with cyber offences

Cyber laws are of utmost importance to curb the menace of cybercrime which has drastically affected the well being of individual and society as a whole. It is a bunch of rules that comply with the established rule of law and guards the interest of every person. On today the number of internet user is over 4.66 billion which is increasing exponentially on an average of 7% per year. By seeing this swift increase in the use of cyberspace, it becomes crucial that proper implementation of cyber rules is there to establish a safe and secured atmosphere for the users. Every single day the internet is developing and becoming highly sophisticated, hence the chances of a surge in online offences is inevitable. Therefore, cyber law acts as a matrix to fully examine the vulnerability of an individual to be victimized in cyber space and provides protection to them. Thus, the importance of cyber law in present scenario cannot be undermined.

\3.3 RELEVANT LAWS SAFEGUARDING THE INTEREST OF WOMEN AGAINST CYBER CRIME

Violence against women or gender-based violence is a very complex, widespread issue of present time and it constitutes as one of the most aggravated form of violation to which women are subjected. Violence against women in our society is not a new concept but it has existed since ages especially with the patriarchal setup. Women from every walk of life are discriminated on gender bases and are subjected to violence such as domestic violence, rape, assault, trafficking in female, forced prostitution, acid attack and many more. Women belonging to specific group suffers various form of discrimination, such as women belonging to marginalized section of society, lesbian, bisexual and transgender women are more vulnerable to violence and harassment.[87] Gender based discrimination is very common, for example, lesbian women face more violence just based on their sexual orientation. Violence against women (VAW) has been a matter of concern for the legislation since ages. Women encounter violence in every sphere of life. The crime against female section has currently raised an alarm with minor girls being subjected to cruelty.

The problem of VAW has gained momentum with the coming of internet. The internet has aggravated the speed of violence that is committed on women and girls in virtual world. Social media sites and internet has served as a safe platform for the perpetrators to victimize male counterpart on large scale and escape prosecution. Cybercrimes especially against women has found a new way to accelerate the growth of VAW to a greater extent. Gender based crimes are getting more prominent in the cyber world. On an average every third women have been victimized in the virtual world. Therefore, it is the need of the hour to have such legal framework which protects the women dignity in the cyberspace and safeguard their interest.

In India we have some legislation which safeguard the rights of women and preserve their dignity in the cyber space. These particularly includes:

- The Constitution of India
- Indian Penal Code, 1860
- The Information Technology Act, 2000
- The Immoral Traffic (Prevention) Act, 1956
- The Indecent Representation of Women (Prohibition) Act, 1986
- POCSO Act, 2012
- Criminal Amendment Act, 2013

The rules enshrined in these acts protect the womanhood from being victimized in any sense in virtual world. The provisions encompassed in the constitution and the other legislation has somehow promoted women welfare and has helped in regulating the activities carried out in cyber space against women. Various cases of cybercrimes against women have been reported in few years which has raised the concern for women safety. The Indian Judiciary and the

---

[87] Violence Against Women-OHCHR, *available at:* https://www.ohchr.org(last visited on June 15, 2021)

Government of India is working towards the safety of women and girl child in the cyber space. Although with the spontaneous evolution of the cyberspace has questioned the legality of the present laws but still the present laws and recent amendment has curtailed the problem of cybercrime against women to certain extent.

3.4 CONSTITUTIONAL PROVISIONS SAFEGUARDING THE INTEREST OF WOMEN

The constitution is regarded as the foundation of democracy. It is the backbone of our Indian culture. Its s often regarded as the sacred book of our nation as it protects the right of every individual and imposes certain duty on them. In other words, it can be said that the constitution is like a river which quenches away the thirst of every citizen without any discrimination. In the ambit of the Indian Constitution, it is clearly stated that every human shall be treated equally and their rights shall be preserved by the states and any violation of basic human right of any individual would lead to penalizing the wrong doer.

The Constitution of India protects the basic human rights of such as right to life, liberty, equal treatment, right to legal aid and right to have justice. It follows the basic principles postulated by the United Nation Human Rights Declaration i.e.to protect the basic human rights of every individual which he is entitled to since birth without any gender biasness.

When we talk about individual rights enshrined in constitution, it simply says everyone shall be treated equally irrespective of gender, caste, creed, sex, etc. But we have seen that biasness on the bases of sex or gender is quite prevalent in our society. Gender based crimes are often been committed, where the female section of the society is more vulnerable to violence then the male section. Crime against women is a huge problem as it can be committed behind four walls of home, in public place, workplace, school, vehicle, etc. Cyber crime against women has further worsen the condition. The cyber-attacks in cyber space against women are rising at an alarming rate. To combat the menace of violation in cyber space against women and girls need to be protected from the perpetrators and for this we need an effective legal mechanism.

The constitution of India has enshrined the basic rights to which women are entitled irrespective of their sex orientation and protect them against crime in any form. The constitutional framework has provided certain rights to women and enforce the duty over states to formulate such laws and policies which look forward to protect the interest of women and provide a better and safe society to live in. It even encompasses certain rights to women while they access the internet facilities. Therefore, the constitutional and legal rights which protect the women in the cyberspace against violence are as follow:[88]

IMPORTANT CONSTITUTIONAL AND LEGAL PROVISIONS FOR WOMEN PROETCTION IN CYBER SPACE

- ARTICLE 14- The principle of gender equality
- ARTICLE 15- State to make special laws for protection of women
- ARTICLE 21- Right to life and liberty viz a viz Right to Privacy
- ARTICLE 23 -24 -Right against exploitation and human trafficking

3.4.1 ARTICLE 14: GENDER EQUALITY

Equality and equal status of law is the main principle which regulate the social set up. In order to establish a well-organized society, it is important that equality in every sphere is maintained. The Indian Constitution recognizes the right to equality as a fundamental right which is bestowed to every citizen. It is enshrined in the constitution that every individual shall be treated equally irrespective of caste, creed, color, religion, gender, and sex orientation. Equality needs to be retained in every sphere of the social activities.

The right to equality and equal treatment embodies the rule that every individual even has right to access technology. At present technology in any form has become part of our daily lifestyle. Among all the technology advancement, internet has covered the vast sphere in of an individual life. When it comes to equal distribution of resources, internet comes at first, as on today every individual have easy access to it. Today, every section of

---

[88] *Supra 30 120*

society is in touch with internet and has ben enjoying all the benefits arising out of it. But, in virtual world the concept of equality seems to narrow.

As on today, we have witnessed a massive increase in the gender-based crime that is taking place in the virtual world. To add to this victimization of women in the cyberspace has increased at par thus questioning the effectiveness of the legal framework. Thereby, the constitution of Indian provides equal representation of all in the eyes of law.

Under Article 14 women have the right to be treated equally irrespective of any religion, caste or sex orientation. It even covers the right of women belonging to LQBTQ section of our society. The provisions enshrined under Article 14 is not just limited to physical world but are also applicable to virtual world. As the crime against women are increasing in the cyber space, it becomes the duty of legislation to treat women equally and address their query on time. Women rights of equal treatment cannot be suppressed on the bases of minority or due to their sex orientation. Women belonging to any section of the society be it a minority section, migrant women, women from well to do family, lesbian or from LGBTQ community, are to be treated equally as provided under Article 14.

If a crime is committed in the virtual world against women, they are entitled to be treated equally before law and according to procedure established by law. The victim of cybercrime needs to be addressed in consonance with the procedure which are established in our Criminal Justice System. Every official while dealing with the case of cybercrime against women need to proceed accordingly as established by the rules and procedure laid down in particular statute. It bestows duty on the state and officials to protect the rights of women who are subjected to violence in virtual world and establishes such rules and regulations to combat the menace of cybercrime against women.

Gender equality in the virtual world is recognized under Article 14 which recognize the equal protection of male counterpart and treat them equally before law. Every act carried out in the virtual space need to be in conformity with the constitutional provisions.

3.4.2 ARTICLE 15: STATE TO MAKE SPECIAL RULES FOR PROTECTION OF WOMEN

Women from all walks of life has made their contribution in all spheres of life and towards the social welfare, but irrespective of this they suffer a lot in silence. There is no doubt that women uphold a special status in present time but behind the curtain they are subjected to violence all around the globe. India is no exception to this. In India women has been given the status of female deity and is represented as "SHAKTI- A Divine Soul". But when we look in depth the female section of our society is tortured and face the brutality of our patriarchal setup. Women are discriminated and are referred as the most disadvantageous section of society.

While the Indian constitution has recognized that women are no less than their counterparts and must be treated equally in every sphere. Empowering womanhood is the key towards a developed and moralistic society. But unfortunately, the female section of our society is subjected to violence. They are beaten up, murdered, raped, forced into prostitution, forced to indulge in illegal sexual activities and what not. Where earlier violence against women was limited to home, has now been extended even in the virtual world. The crime against women in cyberspace is increasing at an accelerated pace, thus, questioning the validity of our legal statutes.

Violence Against Women in the cyberworld has made the female section more vulnerable and more prone to abuse in their social life. **Pandit Jawaharlal Nehru once said - *"To awaken the people, it is the women who must be awakened. Once she is on the move, the family moves, the village moves, the nation moves"*.** In order to outcast the prevailing evils that exist in our society against women it becomes the utmost duty of the government to frame such laws which protects the interest of women in the physical and virtual space.[89]

Gender discrimination in the nation brings cultural, social, economic and educational differences which stops overall growth of the nation. Thus, the most effective remedy to kill the prevailing evils against women in the virtual world it becomes necessary to ensure women protection by ensuring the Right to Equality mentioned in the Constitution of India.

Therefore, Article 15 clearly states that it is the duty of the states to protect the interest of women in every sphere by framing such relevant rules which ever is necessary. In India at present, we have various legislation which ensures that women's rights are protected and they

---

[89] Women Empowerment, available at: *https://www.legalserviceindia.com* (last visited on June15, 2021)

are not subjected to any violence. It even provides that if a state thinks, that a particular legislation is required to combat the menace of crime against women, it is free to do the same.

It embarks a duty on the legislation to uphold the integrity of the nation by farming such laws which are not bias in nature and avoid any gender discrimination. As on today, we have witnessed the trend of cybercrimes that are taking place against women and girls on a large scale. The perpetrators look for an easy way to target women and harass them, and cyberspace acts as a fuel to it. Cybercrime against women such as -women harassment, bullying, trolling, defamation, sexual exploitation of women in cyber space, trafficking and forced sexual orientation, etc. are quite common in the virtual world. To combat such situation there are various statutes and amendment that took place in recent time to combat the situation of cyber violence against women.

SPECIAL PROVISION PROTECTING WOMEN RIGHTS IN CYBER SPACE ARE:

- **CRIMINAL LAW (AMENDMENT) ACT OF 2013** – The criminal amendment act of 2013 which is even referred to (Nirbhaya Act) amened the Indian Penal Code, Evidence Act and Code of Criminal Law in relation to sexual offences. It broadens up the definition of sexual offences and covered in its ambit any kind of sexual offences which takes place against women in the physical world and the virtual world.[90]

- **THE INDECENT REPRESENTATION OF WOMEN (PROHIBITION) ACT, 1986**- This act prohibits publishing of any image of women in newspaper, magazines or on internet in an indecent manner.

- **THE IMMORAL TRAFFICKING (PREVENTION) ACT, 1956** -This act embodies rules and regulations to prohibit trafficking in women and girls which takes place in real and virtual world.

---

[90] Criminal Law (Amendment) Act, 2013, *available at:* https://en.wikipedia.org (last visited on June 16, 2021)

- **THE INFORMATION TECHNOLOGY ACT, 2000-** The IT Act was passed in 2000 and amended in 2008. It specifically deals with the cybercrimes committed against women.

- **PROTECTION OF CHILDREN FROM SEXUAL OFFENCES, 2012:** This act provides an insight to the crimes that takes place against child especially girl child and protect them against the violence and threat in the virtual and physical world.

Apart from these acts, the states are also empowered to formulate legal framework to protect women against violence and make the world both cyber and physical a better place to live.

3.4.3 ARTICLE 21: RIGHT TO LIFE AND LIBERTY vis-à-vis RIGHT TO PRIVACY

Article 21 is regarded as the heart of the Indian Constitution. It is the most pivotal and important provision of the Indian Constitution. It lays down the provisions which work towards forming a progressive nation. The reason why it is considered as the heart of constitution is due to the unlimited rights which it protects within its ambit. It preserves the sanctity of the whole constitution by recognizing the value of an individual life. It recognizes the elementary rights which are required to provide a better life to every individual. In order to provide a better life, it considers certain rights essential and includes-right to liberty, right to food and shelter, right to clean environment, right to education, right to fair trial, right to justice etc. It put emphases on the basic necessity which are prerequisite need of the hour. Recently it has added two more important segment of a peaceful life i.e. Right to Internet and Right to Privacy.

Taking into account the present scenario of increasing trend of internet use, it recognized Right to Internet and Right to Privacy as two important segments of right to life. An important aspect of Art. 21 of the Indian Constitution which includes the word "personal liberty" reveals that for an individual to lead a dignified life in society, his/her liberty should be protected which ultimately demand for the legal recognition to be given to right to privacy. [91] Even the state is bound to respect this right and has a duty to protect life of every individual.

With the ever-growing reliance over internet lead to emergence of crime in the cyber space, it was realized by the Judiciary that it is necessary to incorporate such provision in the constitution which safeguard the life of the users in the virtual world, therefore, it was with this that right to privacy was recognized and was given the status of fundamental right. It protects the users against data infringement or impersonation in cyberspace. In case where the personal information of any person is stolen from his account and is used to commit crime against him/her, then in such case the victim is entitled to invoke their fundamental rights provided under Article 21. It incorporates in its ambit the basic rights which fulfils the righteous way of living a peaceful and dignified life even in the virtual arena.

Article 21 acts as a guardian of the person whose rights are infringed in the cyber world and thus protect the interest of victim by delivering justice to them. Victimization of women in the cyber space is most common such as cyber harassment, sexual assault, bulling, publishing explicit content about women on web, hacking their account, blackmailing etc. These crimes bring disrepute to the dignity of women and injure their reputation in the society. As Article 21 recognizes the right to dignity as an essential part of life, it protects the women dignity and preserve the sanity of womanhood in the cyberspace

❖ THE RIGHT TO PRIVACY

"Man's home is his castle", the aforementioned saying simply applies to the basic inherited right of "Right to Privacy" to which every human being is entitle since his/her birth. Every human has some confidential and secret aspect of their life which they hesitate to represent in the public domain. With the rapid technological advancement in every field

---

[91] *Supra 30 317*

gained the momentum throughout the globe to recognize the right to privacy as a fundamental right of every individual.[92]

Privacy, in its simplest sense, means to have a personal space where an individual is left alone along with his solitude. Privacy is that catalyst of the entire society which needs to be preserved and protected from the outer world, as it's a personal thing of an individual. The right to privacy in a general sense is recognized as a moral right under common law. Although, human shares a great relationship bond with the society, but that doesn't mean that his personal life can be overreached by anyone. Thus, the right to privacy is the purest form of any right bestowed to mankind.

Article 21 recognizes the Right to Privacy as the basic fundamental right to which every person is fully entitled without any discrimination. It is the natural right embodied in the society from the time one is born. The concept of right to privacy gained importance with the rising concern over cybercrime that took place in the virtual world. Privacy in cyberspace is the most sensitive data which is often misused by the cyber criminals and use the personal data of the victim to commit crime such as fraud, online theft, defaming the person, an act of snubbed suitor to take revenge, or any other offence. Data breach is getting very common and this violates the right to privacy of the victim. It is important that cyberspace and the privacy right goes hand in hand to protect the interest of individual.

CYBERSPACE AND RIGHT TO PRIVACY

In present era the two most striking features of our society are: heavy reliance on technology and increasing trend of becoming part of virtual space. Today, the world has gone online turning into a global village of interface and social media. It has connected the world together by a simple network connectivity. We cherish every moment that we spend online having conversation with family and friends. But behind the curtains, internet poses a great threat of crime to the world.

Cyberspace acts as new frontier for gathering personal information about an individual, and over years has grown so powerful that it has started exploiting the users on web.

---

[92] Essay On: Right to Privacy: Its Sanctity In India, *available at: https://ctconline.org >pdf* (last visited on June 16, 2021)

Cyber space acts as a room to breed all forms of cybercrimes taking place around the globe. For instance, in crimes like cyber phishing, where a user shares his credentials but ultimately becomes a victim of cyber fraud.

The internet is rapidly becoming the hub where one can get easy access to personal information of anyone and use the same for unlawful means. Cyber space in general is a non- physical place which is created in the web world by the computers. And internet emergence had made this no- physical space more extravagant to commit cyber offences. Currently, cyber space is being used as core to get the relevant information about the person from his account or computer device without his knowledge, thus violating his /her right to privacy. There are two basic ways through which the perpetrator gathers the personal information of the victim – either through website which directly solicit the personal information of their users, or by hacking their system and account by illegal means.

In Justice K.S. Puttaswamy (Retd) v. Union of India, Hon'ble Supreme Court of India held that 'The right to privacy is protected as an intrinsic part of the right to life and personal liberty under Article 21 and as a part of the freedoms guaranteed by Part III of the Constitution'. Therefore, whenever there is cybercrime and violation in respect of person's private property or his personal belongings or breach of data and identity theft, then the accused can also be charged under Article 21 of the Indian Constitution.[93]

WOMENS RIGHT TO PRIVACY

The Internet and the Web World were largely the great inventions of men. It has enhanced the personal, social and political life of every individual. Today both men and women are designing cyberspace, and both men and women are using it according to their need. The usage of internet and web has developed a culture of going digital. This very culture of going digital entail within its ambit certain serious threat to the community. As digitalization took over the old age ways of carrying out daily routine work it embarked the beginning of criminal offences to take place in cyber space.

---

[93] A.I.R 2017

In past few decades, the cyberspace has emerged as a huge platform to carry out criminal acts against the users. Although people from all of walk of life are facing the brunt of cyber offences, but among all the female section of our society is more vulnerable to become a victim of it. While the cyber space has given recognition to women in business and political sphere, it has even caused hindrance in their privacy right. Women in cyberspace do not enjoy the same level and types of desirable privacy that men do. Women in our society still faces violence today, privacy problems in cyberspace exist there too. The reason behind victimization of women beneath the curtains of cyberspace are that even today they are perceived as inferiors and soft targets to be victimized. In short, the old age social norms of predominance of men over women that we see in real world are also prevalent in the cyber world.

The notion that women are the soft target makes room for the special problem of breach of privacy especially for women. When it comes to breach of privacy, women are more concerned than men, as the personal information which the offender gather from online may be used against them and the society would blame women only in case crime is committed against them.

Article 21 acts as a catalyst which protect women right of privacy in the cyber world. Infringement of privacy is very common in the cyber space as on can easily get the confidential information about the user without his knowledge through illegal access to their computer device. Article 21 has clearly recognized that right to privacy is an important part of right to live with dignity. Every citizen irrespective of gender is fully entitled to right of privacy and the one who infringes or violates this right of others, be it a state part or non-state party shall be liable for being prosecuted under law established. It guarantees the right to privacy to women in the real as well as virtual world.

Where a women confidential information is stolen from her computer device and the same is used against her to victimize her in virtual world by stalking, harassing, blackmailing or forcing her to indulge in any activity which brings disrepute to her dignity, would be covered under Article 21 of Indian constitution. Therefore, right to privacy in the virtual world is a well-established fundamental right to which every woman of the society irrespective of any sex orientation is entitled since birth. Anyone who violates this basic right of women even in the virtual space shall be accountable for criminal liability.[94]

3.4.4 ARTICLE 23-24: RIGHT AGAINST EXPLOITATION AND HUMAN TRAFFICKING IN WOMEN IN CYBER SPACE

Trafficking in human and their exploitation is the third most prominent type of syndicated crime after drug trafficking and illegal transportation of weapon. Human trafficking is defined as the trade practices where the trade of person is done for the purpose of forced labor, committing sexual slavery, or commercial sexual exploitation. Human trafficking is an ever-increasing crime which can occur within the territory of a nation or within different nations.[95] Human trafficking is a crime against humanity and is recognized as an international crime. Women and young girls are more prone to be trafficked across borders and are exploited by the traffickers. They are forced to indulge in illegal sexual activities (prostitution), or used as a commercial sexual product, or are forced to marry by the traffickers.

At present the trafficking of women and girls and their exploitation has turned out to be more common practice with the coming up of internet. Online crimes against women are ever increasing and trafficking of women online has found a new platform. In comparison to traditional way of trafficking of women and girls, the online platform is safer and easy way to carry out trafficking. Online trafficking of women and girls have increased many folds. Social media sites and internet has made it easy for the traffickers to come in contact with the women and young girls and make it easy for them to target particular female and force her to indulge in illegal sexual activities. This could be done by continuously stalking women online and gathering all personal data about those women and use the same credential to locate their place and sell the victim online.

Trafficking of women in India is no exception. Women in India are also traumatized in less obvious ways. The oppression of women starts almost invisibly. One such grave violence to which Indian woken are being subjected is sexual exploitation and trafficking

---

[94] *Ibid 81*
[95] Right Against Exploitation (Article 23-24) Under Indian Constitution, *available at: https://blog.ipleaders.in* (last visited on June 17, 2021)

in the cyber world. Due to patriarchal setup of Indian society, where women are always looked down upon by their counterparts. They are subjected to various forms of cruelty starting from home to public places, and women are expected to be silent and suffer all pain in silence. The suppression of women in our society gives an opportunity to exploit the women in virtual world. The cyber criminals are aware that if a woman is victimized, she would stay quite in every situation. Thus, this has increased the crime of sexual exploitation of women to great extent.[96] It is to be noticed that within no time the trafficking of women from all walks of life be it rich, poor, educated, illiterate or women belonging from LGBTQ community are becoming a soft target for exploitation in cyber space.

One of the most common reasons for trafficking in women in today's time lies with the rising prostitution trade. In the cyber space the traffickers usually promise women to marry them and take them to a destined place, but the truth is that women are often raped and abused by traffickers and make video of such women in a depilated state and post it on web-thus making pornography of the victimized women. While in some cases the traffickers marry the targeted women or girls on faulty grounds and push them into flesh trade world. The trade of selling women and young girls in cyberspace has increase the flesh trade market and significantly effect the social life of such women or girl.

In order to stop this menace of cyber trafficking and sexual exploitation of women in the cyber space Article 23 and 24 of Indian Constitution plays a significant role. Article 23 and 24 protects the right of women and children from being trafficked and exploited. It states any person who indulges in trafficking of human (women or children) shall be held accountable to be penalized in consonance with the afore mentioned articles. Article 23 and 24 protects the women and young girls from being sexually exploited and restrain trafficking of them in real and social world.

It prohibits exploitation of women and young girls in way of forced labor, forced sexual activities, selling or buying of them online, and abusing them. As the cyber menace against women is rising in the cyber space it becomes important that women and young girls are protected in every suitable way. Therefore, the right against exploitation and

---

[96] Women Trafficking In India- A Critical Analyses, *available at: https://www.shanlaxjournals.in* (last visited on June 18, 2021)

human trafficking is the fundamental right to which every woman and young girls are entitled since birth, and even the state is under legal duty to protect the rights of women and girls in the cyber space to make it a safe place for women. Online platform is becoming a hub of such illegal inhumane criminal act which is being carried out against humanity, and therefore it becomes the duty of legal agency to curb this menace and secure the fundamental rights of every individual irrespective of gender biasness.

3.5 RELEVANT PROVISIONS OF INDIAN CRIMINAL JUSTICE SYSTEM DEALING WITH RIGHTS OF WOMEN AGAINST CRIME

In today's techno-savvy environment, the world is getting more advanced and digitally sophisticated. This has widened the scope of cybercrime as well. Initially internet was developed as a research tool and information gathering source. With the passage of time internet became more of what transactional in nature with coming up of e- commerce, e-business, e-governance etc. As the world went for digitalization, the area for cybercrime also widened up. In order to deal with this situation there arises a need to have concrete legal structure to combat cybercrime. All legal issues related to internet crime are dealt with through cyber law. It punishes every sort of crime which is committed against humanity. It is not gender-biased law, rather it recognizes the rights and duty of every individual be it male or female. Under Indian criminal justice system special laws are formulated which specifically protects the women against violence. There are various sections under criminal law which protects the women against crime committed against them in the real and virtual world. It prescribes punishment for the offences which target women in general and exploit them. With the growing concern over victimization of women in cyber space as well has ushered an importance to the protection of women in virtual space and prescribing harsh punishment to the culprit. Under Indian Penal Code and Code of Criminal Procedure women are protected against crimes omitted against them in physical and virtual space.

The provisions laid under the criminal legal system are enacted in consonance with the fundamental rights enshrined under Indian Constitution under Part III-IV. The main principle of the Indian Criminal Justice System is to regulate the behavior of every individual in society so that the sanctity of the constitution is preserved. Every provision enacted under criminal legal system bores a duty to protect the interest of every individual and penalize the offender by protecting his rights to which he is entitled by the virtue of Indian Constitution.

3.5.1 PROVISIONS UNDER INDIAN PENAL CODE SAFEGUARDING WOMEN INTEREST

The Indian Penal Code of 1860 is the backbone of the criminal justice system. Indian Penal Code is an important statute which consist of set of rules and regulations laid down for the operation of a systematic society. It elaborates various offences and prescribe penalties for the same in accordance with the laws laid down. The Indian Penal Code includes all the relevant criminal offences dealing with offences against an individual, the state, offenses against public, offences for armed forces, offences against property, offences against religion, offences against women and children. Indian Penal Code covers all the basic offences which bare committed against individual in any form which affects the society as at large. While with the new technology comes new problems, one such problem is cybercrime. Cybercrime based on gender biasness is prominent issue of present time, and India is no exception to it. We have seen rise in cyber violence against women carried out at a large scale thus affecting the social life of woman in general. Thus, to protect the women against violence in cyber space certain provisions are laid down under Indian Penal Code.[97]

Offences	Punishment
Section 354: Outraging the modesty of	Imprisonment for 1 year which may extend to 5 years and with fine

---

[97] *Indian Penal Code* (45 of 1860)

women	
Section 354 A: Sexual Harassment	Rigorous Imprisonment for s term which may extend up to 3 years, or fine, or with both
Section 354 C: Voyeurism	Imprisonment for not less than 1 year, which may extend up to 3 years and with fine
Section 354 D: Stalking	Imprisonment up to 3 years and fine
Section 366A: Sexual Exploitation	Imprisonment for a term which may extend up to 10 years with fine
Section 366B: Importation of girls	Imprisonment for a term which may extend up to 10 years with fine
Section 372-373: Trafficking	Imprisonment for a term which may extend up to 10 years with fine
Section 463-465: Forgery	Imprisonment for a term which may extend to 2 years with fine, or both
Section 499: Defamation	Punishment of simple imprisonment up to 2 years, fine or both
Section 509: Words, gesture or act to insult modesty of a women	Simple imprisonment for a term up to 3 years and with fine

OUTRAGING MODESTY OF WOMEN IN CYBER SPACE

Modesty is said to be outraged by such an act of offender which shocks the mental state of woman and is recognized as an insult to female decency and dignity.[98] In contemporary time the crime against women has gained significance with the invention of cyber space. Unlike any traditional crimes committed against women, cybercrimes are graver and inflict mental injury to the victimized women. Cyber space has turned out to be a dark

---

[98] Offences Against Women and Provision for It Under IPC, *available at :https://blogpleaders.in*(last visited on June 18, 2021)

web where women modesty is outraged by the culprit by posting some indecent comments or uploading pictures of women in depilated state, thus bringing disrepute to her dignity in society.[99]

Women are insulted in the cyber space by the culprits by exhibiting illicit images of women, or showing such gestures or commenting such words on her personality or character or invading into her privacy without her consent with an intent to molest her and outrage her modesty in the society.[100] Any content which is being published online against any women or younger girls just to outrage her modesty is not between the culprit and the victim , rather it goes public and some times takes a bad shape and turns into violent act such as rape , murder and acid attacks. While such acts affect the mental state of the victim, it even infringes the fundamental rights of women enshrined under Article 21 which talks about right to dignity as a basic right of every individual, including women from every section of society be it rich, poor, educated or from LGBTQ section.

In order to curb the issue of outraging the modesty of women in cyber space and in real world, we have Indian Penal Code which strictly construe with Article 21 and punish the offender with imprisonment and fine, so that the other person before outraging the modesty of women think twice to commit such act.

SEXUAL HARRASSMNET IN VIRTUAL WORLD AND PENALTY FOR THE SAME

The term 'Harassment' is referred to a form of biasness or discrimination. It generally means any unwanted physical act or conduct that offends or humiliates the other person. It covers a wide range of behavioral pattern which is offensive in nature.[101] It is acknowledged as a behavior that is humiliating in nature and embarrasses a person. the act of harassment is not at all reasonable and is not morally accepted by the society. Such behavior has an impact on the mental and physical being of a person who is harassed.

Sexual harassment based on gender discrimination is common in our society. The male counterpart is more prone to sexual harassment at home, workplace, at public places,

---

[99] *Indian Penal Code* (45 of 1850), Section 354
[100] *Indian Penal Code* (45 of 1860), Section 509
[101] What is Sexual Harassment Under Indian Law, available at : *https://www.livemint.in (last* visited on June 18, 2021)

institutions, etc. Sexual harassment against women can be in any form, be it verbally or physically. Today internet and social media are the two main platform on which women faces incidence of sexual harassment. Online sexual harassment consists a wide range of behavioral pattern which uses digital content such as-some images, illicit videos or posting of obscene content online. The impact of sexual harassment varies on the gravity of offences that's inflicted on women. It usually makes the victim feel miserable, threatened, exploited and discriminated among other fellow members.

Cyberspace has become a new place to harass and exploit women. Women faces harassment by the perpetrators now or then on social media platform. Under Indian criminal justice system harassment of women in any way is condemned and the offender is penalized for such act for maximum imprisonment.[102] Sexual harassment of women whether in real world or cyber space is considered as criminal offence and is not acceptable by the law.

PROHIBITION ON CYBER VOYEURISM AGAINST WOMEN:

The Internet invention is the biggest accomplishment of man in all times. It has made the daily life activities easy and time saving. But unfortunately, it serves as a platform for gravest form of cybercrimes that is instituted against women in the virtual world. Voyeurism is one such unnoticed and unreported cybercrime. Voyeurism refers to an act of watching someone while they are engaged in a private act and hold the apprehension that no one watches them as its their personal matter. It included one is intimating with their partner or when any person is changing clothes in a trial room or any private room, where it is expected no one is watching them. Generally, such offences are committed by man towards women to exploit her. Cyber voyeurism is referred to an act of capturing the images or making video of women when they engage in a private act, or place camera in the trial room to exploit the women by intruding into their privacy. This can be done by publishing such images of women on internet which are obscene and indecent. The criminal justice system recognized the act of cyber voyeurism as an offence against women dignity and laid out provisions to punish the offender who engages in such act.[103]

---

[102] *Indian Penal Code* (45 of 1860) Section 354A
[103] *Indian Penal Code* (45 OF 1860) Section 354C

CYBER STALKING AS A CRIMINAL OFFENCE:

Stalking in a general sense is an act of keeping an unwanted surveillance over another person. Basically, the act of stalking is a behavior of following the victim by monitoring there day to day activities and is interrelated with harassment and criminal intimidation against the victim. Stalking behaviors are interrelated to harassment and intimidation and may include following the victim in person or monitoring them.[104]

Stalking is an abrupt behavior of following another person with an intention to cause harm or inflict pain. The traditional way of stalking has been taken over by cyber stalking. The stalkers have found a new platform to monitor the activities of the victim. Women and young girls are more prone to become victim of cyber stalking. Social media sites such as Facebook, Instagram, Twitter and Snapchat are the most common platform used by the users for their entertainment. But these sites are also being used by the perpetrators as an edge to stalk the targeted women or young girls. Cyber stalking involves keeping a vigilant check over the images, posts or other any other content uploaded by the users online. While women and girls are more likely to get exploited by the cyber stalkers, therefore, it becomes necessary to penalize the offence of stalking. Under Indian Penal Law stalking women in any way is criminalized and the offender is punished for the offence of stalking.[105]

SEXUAL EXPLOITATION OF WOMEN AND GIRLS IN CYBER SPACE

Sexual exploitation of women in our society has been there since ages. In earlier times also women were subjected to sexual exploitation and the most common form of

---

[104] Stalking, *available at: https://en.wikipedia.org* (last visited on June 19, 2021)
[105] Indian Penal Code (45 of 1860) Section 354D

exploitation at that time was prostitution. Even today, women are sexually exploited by the male dominating society and are forced into flesh trad. But in recent times the sexual exploitation of women has changed its pattern and medium. Today when we talk about the exploitation of women in the cyber world, it is not just limited to internet porn. The exploitation of women via Internet has been carried out in different forms such as trafficking of women, cyber staking, blackmailing, forcing them to indulge into illegal sexual activities or force them into drug trafficking and many such crimes.

Sexual exploitation through cyber space poses a great risk to women and young girls. Internet has made it easy to exploit the women and young girls online, as it is safer and easier to hide their identity. Internet has served a new way of importing young girls from different nations to India from destitute areas, who are forced into flesh trade. Although importation of young girls is recognized as an offence in India and such an act is punishable according to law established.[106] Therefore, the act of sexually exploiting women and importing young girls for same purpose is criminal in nature and the offender is punished for the committing such act.

TRAFFICKING OF WOMEN AND YOUNG GIRLS

Trafficking of human is recognized as an offence against humanity. It violates the human rights which a person is entitled to since birth. Trafficking of women and young girls are of major concern at present and with the internet services the commission of such crime has increased at par. Cyber space has acted as safe place to carry trafficking in women and young girls without any fear. Girls who are minor and women belonging to marginalized section are easy to target and influence, thus, leading to their victimization in cyber world. Trafficking of women and girls is recognized as a criminal offence worldwide. Trafficking of women in particular is done to sexually exploit them and get monetary benefit out of it. Women in cyber world are trafficked by making false promises to them of getting a good job at abroad and then forced into prostitution. Thus, resulting into exploitation of them at the hands of perpetrators.

The Indian criminal justice system recognizes the act of trafficking women and young girls as a criminal offence in consonance with article 23-24bof Indian constitution and

---

[106] Indian Penal Code (45 of 1860) Section 366B

prescribes imprisonment for a term which may extend up to 10 years.[107] The punishment prescribed for cyber trafficking of women and young girls is rigorous in nature, in order to set an example for others and is expected to have a deterrent effect in the society to avoid exploitation of women in virtual world.

FORGERY OF DOCUMENTS

Forgery means making false document of someone with an intent to cause damage to another person. Forgery is an offence of gathering personal information about another person and making false document on that base either in electronic form or by other means, in order to cause damage to person or property. By making forged document, the main aim of the culprit is to cause damage to the victim by forcing him to indulge in any malicious acts which causes damage to the other person.[108] In cyber space it is easy to get information about the victim through illegal access to their accounts or devices by hacking them and create a false identity on their names. The act of forgery in cyber space is directly related to infringement of privacy.

Forged document can be made easily against women and young girls by collecting all information from their online accounts and create a fake identity of it and use the same commit any crime, which brings disrepute to them in society. By creating false identity, the culprit usually blackmails the victim and force them to indulge into any illegal activity. In cyber space fake accounts in the name of other person are created by the culprit to carry illegal acts by hacking their accounts and getting all information about the targeted victim. Creating false account of women ad young girls on social media sites without their knowledge is very common. The perpetrator uses the fake accounts to carry illegal acts in the name of targeted women or girl to cause injury to her reputation. The act of collecting information without the consent of the victim and using the same against them by creating a false identity is recognized as a criminal act under Indian Penal Code and the offender is punished for the same.

---

[107] *Indian Penal Code* (45 of 1860) Section 372
[108] *Indian Penal Code* (45 of 1860) Section 463

CYBER DEFAMTION

Defamation is an act of publishing any content about someone either in written form or verbal form to bring disrepute or cause injury to his/her reputation. Similarly, when such an act is committed in the cyberspace through internet medium it is called Cyber Defamation. With the rise in usage of internet and social media platform the act of cyber defamation is also increasing. The offender uses online platform to publish such content that is offensive and would injure the reputation of the victim. Cyber defamation includes- publishing false information in an advertisement form, posting of any images, or using abusive or harsh words in comment section.

Cyber defamation is the most common offence which is committed against women to tarnish her image in the society. Usually, cyber defamation against women is committed by the snubbed shooter to satiate vengeance. Cyber defamation against women can have grave impact on the mental state of the victimized women. It can affect their personal and social life to great extent. In order to resolve this issue of defamation be it in real world or virtual world, we have criminal justice system which recognizes the act of defamation as an offence until and unless it is done in good faith or for public welfare.[109] It is a gender biased offence which is carried out against women and girls, so therefore to avoid any discrimination based on gender the Indian Penal Code has established it to be a criminal offence irrespective of being committed against any member of society.

3.6 CRIMINAL AMENDMENT ACT OF 2013:

Criminal Amendment Act of 2013 widened the ambit of certain criminal offences which were not recognized earlier. It widens the scope of sexual offences which were committed against women in society but were not recognized by the law of the land. The Act in particular recognized a broad range of sexual crimes that were committed against women and illustrated how the gender-based crimes manifest the discrimination itself. It defined crimes such as acid attack, voyeurism, cyber stalking, sexual exploitation of women in cyberspace and assault against women. The criminal amendment of 2013 added new provisions to Indian Penal Code, Code of Criminal Procedure and Indian Evidence Act.[110]

---

[109] *Indian Penal Code* (45of 1860) Section 499

The main aim behind this criminal amendment act was to cover all types of violent act to which women in our society are being subjected to due to the gender-based set up in our community. By bringing every act which outrages modesty of women into the ambit criminal law and prescribing punishment for the same lead to covering every malicious act to which females in our society experience due to the male dominant aspect. It even provided for holding the police or other official liable in case they fail to register complaint of victim. Thus, the act by broadening the coverage of criminal's acts committed against women in real and virtual world, lead to formulating a strong and efficient criminal justice system which seek to promote justice to the victimized women and protect her interest at large.

3.7 STATUTES DEALING WITH PROTECTION OF WOMEN IN VIRTUAL WORLD

Crime against women is ever increasing in our society, and in order to protect the interest of women and guard them against any exploitation it becomes evident to have statutes which especially deals with women interest. At present the female section of our society is becoming more vulnerable to cyber-attacks. Women in cyber space are becoming more vulnerable to exploitation, sexual violence, threat, cyber defamation and most prominent their trafficking and forced prostitution. To curb the victimization of women and young girls in cyber space we have certain legislation which specifically are construed to protect the women against exploitation and preserve their dignity as per provisions of constitution. Some of the legal statutes dealing with protection of women against exploitation are:

- IMMORAL TRAFFICKING (PREVENTION) ACT, 1956
- THE INDECENT RERESENTATION OF WOMEN (PROHIBITION) ACT, 1986
- PROTECTION OF CHILDREN FROM SEXUAL OFFENCES (POCSO) ACT, 2012

- **THE IMMORAL TRAFFICKING (PREVENTION) ACT OF 1956:**

---

[110] Criminal Law (Amendment) Act,2013: Sexual Offences -Academike, available at : https://www.lawctopus.com (last visited on June 20,2021)

Exploitation of women in our society is being practiced since ages. Even in the 21st century the female section is subjugated to exploitation by sexually harassing them or to the worse forcing them into flesh trade business. Today no society is immune to it rather it is plagued with it. Looking at present scenario, every country in the world is directly affected by trafficking in general and prostitution in particular as a crime against women. Although the concept of prostitution is as old as human civilization, but as on today the menace of trafficking of women and girls into flesh trade has grown with the invention of internet. Cyber space has provided a far better and safer way to carry out trafficking in women at an ease.

Today every civilized society and Government has come together to curb this menace of women exploitation, but at large it's not easy to fully eliminate it from society. Yet, the government are putting their efforts to regulate the conduct of these criminals in real world and virtual space by underlying some strict provisions. At present there are adequate number of legislations to prevent the abuse of women by trafficking them and forcing into prostitution. Efforts are being made to regulate the profession of trafficking of women by providing penal measures to protect the interest of women.[111]

The domestic legislation which deals which the prevention of trafficking in women and importation of girls from other nations is knowns as Immoral Trafficking (Prevention) Act of 1956. The present statute deals with trafficking of women in the real world or through cyber space and prescribe the amount of penalty and fine in relation to committing the offence of buying and selling women for monetary benefit. It even recognizes the act of commercial prostitution where women are forced into flesh trade as a criminal offence and prescribe punishment for the same. The main concern behind enacting such legislation is to preserve human dignity, promote the welfare of the individual especially keeping in view the condition of women in society and work for their empowerment. The act also keeps a check over the law enforcing agency whether they work according to the said provision or not.

The present statute criminalizes the commercialization of sexual exploitation of women and their trafficking in general. The relevant provisions under the statute differentiate between forced prostitution and a self -acquired profession of prostitution. It marks a thin line of distinction between the two and punishes those offenders who forcefully indulges women or young girls into prostitution. Though with the rampant technological development in cyber

---

[111] An overview of Immoral Traffic (Prevention) Act,1956, *available at:* https://thedailyguardian.com(last visited on June 20,2021)

space the exploitation of women is far more then reported. Therefore, the present act attempts to curb the menace of women trafficking and forced prostitution in the society and virtual world too.

- ## THE INDECENT REPRESENTATION OF WOMEN (PROHIBITION) ACT, 1986

The statute by its name clearly states the main aim behind enacting particular legislation. It generally regulates advertising such images of women either in magazine, booklets, in form of video, or posting such images which of women online which are indecent in nature. Internet is being used as a medium by these advertising agencies to publish any article, image or other content to get monetary benefit without putting much effort. Initially, the companies use internet platform to advertise their product at low cost and get good amount in return. But in last few years, the cyber space is more prone to victimize women and publish their obscene images as an advertising content to get more pecuniary benefit.

To combat with the cyber offences against women in the web the government passed the Indecent Representation of Women (Prohibition) Act regulates and prohibits the indecent representation of women through the media of advertisements, publications etc. Later on, the Indian Legislation proposed an amendment in the present statute by insertion of The Indecent Representation of Women (Prohibition) Amendment Bill, 2012 which seeks to broaden the scope of the law to cover in its ambit the audio-visual media and content in electronic form, and also included the distribution of material on the internet platform and the way in which women image is portrayed on the web.

The images published by the agencies which outcast the indecent representation of women in the virtual world might ignite hate crime against such women or may cause injury to their reputation. Moreover, publishing of such indecent images of women have adverse effect on the social order and wellbeing. Such images arouse the chance of increase in sexual crimes against women in our society and making it unsafe for them to live in. Therefore, it becomes important to have an efficient legal structure which not only prohibit such activities but even formulate policies for social welfare of every individual especially the female sect of our society. As we know that women are more vulnerable to get victimized in the outer world by such indecent representation of their image in virtual world.[112] To avoid the further exploitation of women in the virtual world, the present act was enacted to prohibit the publication of such images or content about women which is indecent and morally inappropriate for our social order. In India itself women are regarded as "Devi" and to maintain the divine picture of womanhood in our society it is necessary that women are represented in a moral and sophisticated manner to avoid any crime or exploitation of women at home and in society as well. Thus, this act attempts to achieve these goals and promote welfare of women.

- ## THE PROTECTION OF CHILDREN FROM SEXUAL OFFENCES (POCSO)ACT, 2012

The POCSO ACT OF 2012 is one of the important legal statute of Indian criminal justice system which was especially enacted to protect the children from sexual exploitation. It lays down stringent provisions to inflict harsh punishment on the offender who exposes the child to any sexual offense or use them for commercial sexual trade. It is considered as an extra ordinary statute as under it the 'burden of proof' lies on the accused and unlike the IPC provisions the accused is not considered innocent until proven guilty.[113]From the very beginning of crime against child the offender is considered as guilty and it is on him to prove his innocence and his intent. It lays down provisions for grievous breach of fundamental rights of child below the age of 16 and punishes the accused for sexually exploiting them

The procedure laid down under the particular act differ from the Code of Criminal Procedure, as it is child friendly and establishes special court for trial of such cases which fall under the act.[114] It protects the child against sexual violence in cyber space. Today, most of the youth are very active on social media sites and using online tools for gaming,

---
[112] *The Indecent Representation of Women (Prohibition) Act* of 1986
[113] *Ibid*
[114] *POCSO ACT* (13 of 2013) Sectionn28

shopping and doing other activities. They lack awareness about the cybercrimes and often fall victim to the cyber-attacks. The young girls are more vulnerable to become victim of the cyber crimes as they are soft target for the offenders. In past few years, we have witnessed a surge in crime against child be it from rape, sexual harassment, trafficking, child pornography, etc. To protect the innocent child from getting into wrong hands, it becomes important to have such laws which promote their welfare and punishes the offender by establishing special courts for speedy trial. Therefore, the POCSO Act of 2012 was enacted to fulfill the same.

The POCSO Act, lays down provisions which define the offences and prescribe punishment for the same. It punishes the offender to carry out sexual harassment of cyber pornography against young child especially young girls who are more prone to be victimized and sexually exploited.[115] It even prohibit exposing child into pornography trade and flesh trade business which is becoming a common factor contributing to crime against child.[116] The act attempts to combat the menace of the crime against child and promote their safety and welfare in the real and virtual sphere. Moreover, it provides for the law agencies to be more friendly while handling the cases where child is molested as it has an adverse impact on the mental health of the child. Therefore, the act lays down provisions for providing proper care and protection of the child who is victimized and provide medical care in such case where required. To put in one word, the POCSO Act is regarded as the "Friend" of the child who serves for their betterment and upliftment in the society and work for maintain social order in society to protect them against any exploitation in virtual world as well.

3.7 THE INFORMATION TECHNOLOGY ACT, 2000

The birth of internet services changed the earlier way of business transaction by bringing e- commerce into existence. The companies started using internet services to enhance their business and gain benefit of it. While with passage of time the world was going online and digitalization was seen in the European and Western countries, India to adopted this concept and today in 21st century we have digitalized machinery to carry our day-to-day e-transaction. While the e-commerce was gaining momentum, the Ministry of

---

[115] *POCSO ACT* (13 of 2013) Section 13
[116] *POCSO ACT* (13 of 2013) Section 14

Commerce Department formulated first draft to regulate e-transaction and was known as E-Commerce Act, 1998.Later on it was redrafted by the department and passed the bill named "Information Technology Bill of 199" which came into force in May and was officially kwon as Information Technology (IT)Act of 2000.[117]

The Information Technology Act, 2000 provides legal recognition to the transaction done which is carried out online through various electronic devices generally used for communication. It even regulates all online transaction that take place in the virtual mode by debit card, credit card and even gave legal recognition to digital- signature to make e-business transaction easy and reliable. Apart from regulating e- commerce and business transaction that takes place online it even outlaw the old and repugnant laws to curb the menace of cybercrime.

The scope of IT Act of 2000 is not just limited to regulating the e-commerce but it has an important role in criminal justice system also. With the coming up of internet and social media sites the citizens are becoming more tech savvy then ever before and this gave rise to certain malpractices in cyber space. Various instances such as mob lynching, hate crimes, publishing fake information, bullying and exploiting the users in cyberspace are common practices which certainly has an adverse effect on their social life. In order to regulate the conduct of netizens in cyber space and make it a safe place for inter-communication without any interference in their personal life, there was a need for cyber rules and regulations to eliminate cyber offences. Thus, the Government of India put forth the IT Act where certain rules and procedures are enshrined to eliminate the cyber offences. It even eased the work of investigating authority by giving legal recognition to e-evidence and e-discovery to solve criminal cases. It even ruled out certain provisions which exclusively deals with cybercrime and prescribe punishment for the same.

- **PROVSIONS UNDER IT ACT SAFEGUARDING INTEREST OF WOMEN**

Today cyberspace has become a new tool in the hands of criminals to carry all sorts of malpractices without being caught. They ate quite active on social media sites and

---

[117] The Information Technology Act, 2000: Objectives and Features, *available at;* https://www.toppr.com (last visited on June 20, 2021)

other communication networking sites to give color to their illegal activities. In present time, we have noticed a sudden surge in the cases of cybercrimes against women and young children especially girls in the virtual world. With rapid advancement in the IT sector, the criminals use new tactics to victimize the women and exploit them in real and virtual world. Therefore, it comes important for the law enforcing agencies to lay down certain provisions which protect the entity of women in cyberspace and promote their welfare even in the cyber world. The IT Act lays down some of the provisions safeguarding the interest of women in our community in consonance with the Indian Constitution. The provisions are as follow:[118]

Section 66A: Sending offensive messages through communication services	Punishment for a term which may extend to 3 years and with fine
Section 66C: Identity Theft	Imprisonment which may extend up to 3 years or with fine which may extend to one lakh rupees or both
Section 66D: Cheating by personation	Imprisonment which may extend up to 3 years and shall also be liable for fine which may extend to one lakh rupees
Section 66E: Violation of privacy	Imprisonment which may extend up to 3 years and shall also be liable for fine up to one lakh rupees
Section 67A: Publishing or transmitting obscene material in electronic form	Imprisonment for a term which may extend up to 5 years and also with fine which may extend up to ten lakh rupees.
Section 67B: Publishing or transmitting obscene material depicting children	Imprisonment for a term which may extend up to 5 years and fine up to ten lakh and in case of subsequent offence

[118] The Information Technology Act, 2000

	imprisonment up ton 7 years with fine of ten lakh rupees
Section 72: Breach of confidentiality and privacy	Imprisonment for 2 years with fine which may extend up to one lakh

The aforementioned sections were subsequently added to the Information Technology Act of 2000 by the Information Technology (Amendment) bill of 2008. These provisions were added into the IT Act of 2000 by keeping in view the increasing number of cybercrimes that took place in recent times. The act laid down provisions to protect the women and young girls from being exploited in the cyberspace. Let's understand how these sections protect the women interest in the virtual space.

- **PROHIBITION ON SENDING OF OBSCENE MESSEGAES TO WOMAN**

    Internet has become a hub of information, where one can get valuable content just with a click. But it has also been used by the perpetrator to transmit such content to the users which is obscene and indecent in nature. The offender uses social media sites as medium to commit crime against its user. They use computer devices or other communicating devices to send any message, images or upload any post on internet which might be offensive and illegal. The following act prohibit sending or circulating any such message to any women which is obscene and is sexually explicit [119]Although later on this section was held unconstitutional by the court as it violated the rights enshrined under Article 19(2) of Indian Constitution.

- **IDENTITY THEFT**

    Identity theft in cyberworld is quite common, where the hacker generally hacks the account of the user for committing malicious act in particular. Identity theft is a criminal act of stealing someone personal information to commit fraud. Identity thief's area increasingly relying over the use computer technology in order to gather all personal information about other people to commit fraud.

---

[119] *IT Act (*21 of 2000) Section 66A

To commit identity theft the perpetrator usually uses illegal access to get the information about the victim such as by way of hacking their accounts, uses information -gathering malware which infect the computer or use misleading emails or links to get all credential about victim. Identity theft in cyberspace has been ever increasing and is far more likely to affect the women users. The cyber criminals hack the account of women without their knowledge and collect the sensitive information about them and further uses the same to create fake accounts of such women and carry illegal or offensive acts prohibited under criminal justice system. The IT Act lays provisions to protect the personal data and punishes the offender for illegally collecting any personal information of women through illegal access.[120]

- **CHEATING BY PERSONATION:**

Personation is an act where one person uses fake identity of other individual to deceive the other party. Cyber personation is one way by which the perpetrator commit crime against the internet users. The common platform used by the criminals to commit cyber - personation is social media sites such as Facebook, Twitter, Telegram etc., where the perpetrator usually creates false identity to communicate with the users and build up good relations with them and gain their trust. With the identity theft the perpetrator creates fake accounts on these social media sites and communicate with other and generally gather personal information about them and later on might use the same to commit cyber fraud.

Women and young children especially young girls are cheated online by creating personated image on social media. The cyber criminals sometime hack the data of companies and create fake account of such companies and offer job opportunity to women and gain confidence of women and get all personal information about them. After gathering all relevant information by personation, the cyber offender might victimize the women and exploit her in the virtual and real space. Thus, to protect the women against cheating by personation the IT Act punishes the offender who represent himself with false identity in order to deceive another person.[121]

- **VIOLATION OF PRIVACY:**

---

[120] IT Act (21 OF 2000) Section 66C
[121] IT Act (21 of 2000) Section 66D

As enshrined in Indian Constitution every citizen has a right to privacy irrespective of any gender discrimination. Right to privacy has been recognized as a fundamental right to which every individual is entitled since birth. While the constitution has given the status of fundamental right to "Privacy", yet data breach and privacy infringement is a common factor constituting cybercrime in virtual space. Infringement of privacy has been recognized as the main cause for victimization of women in the cyberspace. The cyber offender commits privacy infringement by stealing all personal data about the victim through illegal access to their computer devices. Privacy is an important part of human dignity and it is the duty of legislation to preserve it by regulating the behavior of the internet users and punishes those who violate any provision of the Act with the prescribed penalty. The IT Act recognizes the importance of privacy in the cyberspace and punishes those who infringes the right to privacy of the user and exploit the victim by committing cyber offence against them.[122]

- **PROHIBITION ON PUBLISHING OR TRANSMITTING ANY OBSECENE MATERIAL ONLINE THROUGH ELECTRONIC MEDIA:**

Internet and social media sites were particularly designed for inter-communication between individual from different part of the world. But gradually this platform became a source of medium to commit all sorts of crime. The old way of committing crime traditionally now shifted to online mode. Now crime especially against women are carried online. The culprit exploits the women in cyber space by publishing her nude images, transmitting pornography online, or publishing any such obscene content online which is outrages the modesty of women in virtual and real world. Publishing such content online or transmit to others through computer devices or through other electronic devices which consist of explicit sexual images of women or children is criminal in nature and is prohibited by cyber law and the offender is given harsh punishment to deter such act in future.[123]

---

[122] IT Act (21 of 2000) Section 66E
[123] IT Act (21of 2000) Section 67A

- **PROHIBITION ON PUBLISHING ANY INDECENT MATRIAL ONLINE DEPICTING CHILDREN:**

Young children especially young girls are no immune to cyber offences. At present the younger generation are more active user of internet services and spend their most of their time online specially on social media sites. Due to lack of knowledge about the corrupt world outside and being more emotionally unstable at such tender age make them prone to fall prey in the hands of criminals. Online platform is serving as a curse for children at present as they are becoming victim to hostility and exploitation at large. While young girls are more vulnerable to be victimized and sexually exploited in the cyber space. Crime against children is ever increasing and includes drug trafficking, forced labor, trafficking of young children especially girl child, child pornography, sextortion, indulging them into online illicit activities, etc. Online exploitation of children by making child pornography is main source for bullying in society and on social media sites, therefore, to protect these children rights and curb the menace of cyber crime against them IT Act of 2000 prohibit the publication of any indecent content which describes a child and inflict harsh punishment on the offender.[124]

- **BREACH OF CONFIDENTIALITY AND PRIVACY**

Online breach of confidentiality and privacy are the area which need to be kept secret by the companies, various agencies, institutions and the social networking sites about its customer and users. The companies or the social media sites such as Facebook, Twitter, WhatsApp, Instagram, Snapchat etc. are under obligation to protect the personal information about their users and protect their right to privacy. Although the policies of these companies are regulated under the Indian Contract Act and other relevant statutes, but still the breach of confidentiality and privacy infringement is common in virtual space. The companies who carry out its business online are under obligation to not to share any detail about their worker and their customers availing their services to any outsider. Even in government sector it is the duty of the official to keep all the records,

---

[124] IT Act (21 of 2000) Section 67B

documents and files properly under proper surveillance and the confidentiality must be retained.

But sometimes the hacker might corrupt the computer of the private companies and even the government department computers and by malware or virus attack steal all the relevant information about the victim. In such situation these companies are not held bound for breach of confidentiality. While there are certain instances where the companies shared the personal data about their worker and customer such as their address, email id, phone number and other credentials with other for monetary gain. The perpetrator after getting the relevant information about the victim might target them and exploit them mentally and financially by blackmailing them. This way the crime gets deep into our system and disturb the social order. Data breach in case of women is more prevalent than the male section of society.

Therefore, to uphold the accountability of companies for preserving confidentiality and protecting the right of privacy of the users, the IT Act of 2000, punishes those who deliberately share stored data, or share any record kept, documents or file with other person for certain political or financial gain and levy criminal charges against them for breach of trust and confidentiality and protect the interest of the users.[125]

3.8 LIABILITY OF INTERMEDIATOR

Due to constant development of internet services world has witnessed a drastic change in their overall lifestyle. Today internet service is not just limited to research field or for individual entertainment, rather it has expanded its scope by bringing e-commerce into market. With the increase usage of internet services for commercial purpose and for entertainment, the horizon of internet landscape has drastically changed, thus, giving rise to a new industry called as Internet Service Provider.

Since the advent of internet services, the global witnessed a dramatic change in the way the world was getting connected through online and opened doors for people from different part of world to come together at one place. Today retailers and publisher are flocking online

---

[125] IT Act(21 of 2000)Section 72

platform where they are receiving good response from another end. But sadly, this platform is also not immune from criminal conspiracy. The criminals tend to find new ways and medium to conspire and commit crime either against an individual, state or any firm. Cybercrime has emerged as a global problem for every nation. To commit offence in cyber space basic structure of internet and internet affiliated services are required.

The Internet intermediaries or Internet Service Provider is the one who provide internet's basic infrastructure and platform to the users by enabling communication and transaction between third parties.[126] As the scope of internet and social media sites got widened up so did the role of internet service provider got more prominent. Today, the Internet Intermediator has a significant role to play in thus digitalized era where internet has penetrated deep into our society.

Basically, Intermediaries includes a wide range of online activities such as work of Internet Access and Service Providers (ISPs), net banking system, internet search engines and portals, e-commerce transactions, data processing, web hosting and many more. It provides a channel through which one communicates with other or carry any online transactions. While the internet intermediators have a role to play in disseminating information about their policies and regulations, the very basic question which comes into our mind is whether the internet intermediator has certain liability in cyber space or not? The answer to this question is both yes as well as no to certain extent. Yes, in case where they deliberately share confidential information and no where they are unaware of the fact that the platform provided by them to use internet was used to carry cybercrime irrespective of taking due diligence of their duty.

When any content is disseminated on internet the liability of intermediator is bound to arise as he provides the basic infrastructure to internet and its services. For instance, when any content is published or transmitted via internet which has the tendency to violate the privacy of any person or exploit him or her in cyberspace, then the liability of intermediator is bound to arise. In cyber offences such as cyber defamation, disseminating fake information or publishing hatred content which might bring unrest in society, the role of intermediator comes into question. One of the main reasons behind the liability of internet intermediator for

---

[126] Definition, Role, Function, Internet Service Provider, available at : *http://diarycomputer.blogspot.com* (last visited on June 21, 2021)

any illegal act carried on internet arises as he possesses sufficient knowledge about such publication and has a control over information distributed on internet.[127]

Online intermediaries act as a bridge between the internet and its user. They provide users with necessary facilities and essential services which ultimately make the usage of the internet easy and possible in manner of connecting with people through various sites, carry out different online transactions, gather information from web page and other important online activities. They play a crucial role in virtual space by providing a structured platform which helps individual to communicate through cyber space. Although their liability arises in cases where breach of privacy in cyber space takes place.

In India the term Internet Intermediator is defined under Information Technology (Amendment)Act of 2008 which says that: any person who stores or transmit any information on behalf of another person or provides any internet service with respect to it and generally includes telecom service provider, network service provider, internet service provider, web-hosting service provider, search engines, online payment sites, online-market places and cyber cafes.[128] The online intermediator provides a channel for the subscriber to use and communicate with people. But as we know that cybercrime is on surge mainly cyber defamation, privacy infringement, data breach, publishing of obscene material online and many more the liability of intermediator arises. In Indian the liability of intermediator is brief defined under IT (Amendment) Act of 2008 and is also regulated by virtue of Information Technology (Intermediatory Guidelines) Rules, 2011.

- **GENERIAL LIABILITIES OF INTERMEDIATOR UNDER INFORMATION TECHNOLOGY (INTERMEDIATORY GUIDELINES) RULE OF 2011**

The Information Technology (Intermediatory Guidelines) Rules ,2011 lay down a set of liabilities in Rule 3 under the headline of "Due Diligence". The liabilities enshrined under the rule need to be followed by all the intermediaries who provides the internet infrastructure to

---
[127] *Ibid*
[128] Section 2(1) (w) IT (Amendment)Act ,2008

the subscribers all over India in compliance with section 75 of IT (Amendment) Act of 2008.The rules required to be followed by the intermediaries are as follow:[129]

- **LIABILITY TO FURNISH POLICY GUIDELINES IN CONSONANCE WITH INFORMATION TECHNOLOGY ACT:**

1.It is the foremost duty of the intermediatory to publish rules and regulations for privacy policy and user agreement concerning usage of intermediator computer resources by any person.

2.The intermediator is bound to inform its users in case their non-compliance with the rules and regulations, user agreement and private policy the intermediator has the right to terminate their services and remove non-compliant information.

3.The intermediator is certainly bound to follow the provisions laid down under the Act for time being in force.

4.When required by law, during any investigation of any cybercrime, the intermediator shall fully assist the officer in charge and provide all relevant documents and records as required by such officer.

5.In cases relating to issue of cyber security, the intermediator shall report incidence of cyber security with the Indian Computer Emergency Response Team.

6.The intermediatory shall not intentionally attach or pre-install the technical configuration of computer resources or make any change in the infrastructure which provide internet services to the subscriber for the purpose of obtaining personal information about the user unless and until required by lawful order from officer in charge or authority sited.

---

[129] *Supra 24 157*

7. The intermediator shall publish the name and number of the Grievance Officer on its website, in case any victim suffers from any violation of his privacy rights or matter concerning data breach from their computer devices. The Grievance Redressal officer shall take cognizance of such complaint and redress the issue specified in complaint within a period of one month from the date of receiving such complaint.

- **LIABILITY TO REMOVE SUCH CONTENTS FROM WEBSITE WHICH ARE INDECENT IN ITS NATURE:**

1. The intermediators are under obligation to inform the users of computer resources not to upload, publish, display, transmit or forward any such information or content that (a) belongs to other person without his knowledge and (b) which is obscene, harmful, harassing in nature, pornographic, pedophilic, personal data of any individual, which is hateful, racially discriminatory, gender biased, derogatory, objectionable and unlawful in manner which has a tendency to (c) harm the dignity of a women, child, or infringes any copyright or other proprietary right or (d) which violates any law for time being in force and creates unrest in the society (e) impersonate another person by stealing identity, (f) which destroys the computer system through virus hoax (g) or publishing such content which results into cyber warfare and might result into threatening the very foundation of unity, integrity and sovereignty of India and creates tension between India and foreign states or prevents lawful investigation of any offence which malign the dignity of our nation.[130]

2. The rules prohibit the intermediatory from intentionally publishing such information or sharing such content or modify any such information which might create tension in the society.

3. The intermediatory, on whose system any information is stored or published without his knowledge, and upon bringing it into his knowledge by the victim who got affected, shall within 36 hours work with user or owner of such content to remove it from the site and further preserve the same information for at least 90 days

---

[130] *Supra 24 174*

in case investigation takes place and submit the same to the investigation officer when asked for.

4. The intermediator shall terminate the access to internet services in case the accessor violates any rules and regulations enlisted in the policy published by the intermediator before providing service.

- **LIABILITY TOWARDS PROTECTION OF PRIVACY**:

It is the liability of the intermediator to protect the privacy of the users. The rules enshrined under IT Act guidelines states that the intermediator shall take all necessary steps to secure its computer resources and data stored therein by following all relevant security practices and procedure laid down in Information Technology (Reasonable Security Practices and Sensitive Personal Information) Rules,2011. By virtue of this act, the intermediator is under obligation to protect the sensible information about its users such as passwords, email ids, transaction details, bank account details, contact list, friend list of social media sites, health condition, sexual orientation etc. All of the aforementioned information is covered under sensible information and it becomes the primary duty of the intermediators to preserve this information and maintain privacy. Secondly, it is the duty of intermediator to frame such policies and publish the same regarding the privacy of its users.

The liabilities vested on the intermediaries may show up when seen from the perspective of exploitation of women in the cyber space, thus, raising the apprehension about the liabilities and includes prohibition on publication of any content which may bring disrepute to women and malign her character in society. Therefore, the present guidelines of IT Act give right to women to bring charge against the service providers especially the social media platform when they refuse to provide help to the women who is victimized and exploited on these networking sites. It is the duty of intermediatory or the body corporate to protect the privacy of the users and in any case, they fail to do so their liability arises arise by way of civil tortuous liability or under criminal liability for breach of confidentiality. The civil liability of the body corporate is covered under Section 43 of IT Act ,2000 and the criminal penal liability is covered by section 72A of IT Act, 2000.[131] They are immune from their liability only when a reasonable ground is established by intermediatory in court of law.

3.9 ROLE OF GOVERNMENT IN PROTECTING RIGHT OF INDIVIDUAL IN CYBER SPACE

With the constant growth in the Information Technology sector, India witnessed a sudden jump in the number of subscribers of internet service. India is the third largest user of internet service in the world. With this rampant growth in IT sector and development in the internet services poses a great threat of criminal malpractices in the cyber space thus challenging the legal framework. In past few years the number of online frauds, sexual exploitation of women and young children, data breach and other unlawful activities have caught the attention of the government as it causes unrest in the social order. The Government of India has taken some measures to regulate the activities of individual, government firm or of corporate sector in the cyber space and has formulated certain privacy policy to protect the individual rights.

3.9.1 STEPS TAKEN BY GOVERNMENT OF INDIA TO CURB CYBER CRIME:

1. Central Government has taken steps to spread awareness about cybercrimes among masses by issuing advisories to various departments to make people aware about relevance of cyber security.

2. The government has issued advisories to the law enforcement agency to provide efficient training to the investigating agency and enhance the cyber forensic mechanism to prevent cybercrimes from occurring.

---

[131] *Information Technology Act*, 2000

3. The Government has launched the online cybercrime reporting portal- www.cybercrime.gov.in to facilitate the reporting of complainant mechanism especially pertaining to Child Pornography/Child Sexual Abuse Material, rape/gang rape imageries or publishing sexually explicit content on internet. To handle the issue of cybercrimes in the country The Central Government has formulated a comprehensive scheme for establishing The Indian Cyber Crime Coordination Centre (I4C) which assist and aid in combating cybercrime problem.[132]

Further, Government has taken several initiatives to prevent cybercrime and mitigate cyber security incidents. These include:[133]

1. Establishment of National Critical Information Infrastructure Protection Centre (NCIIPC) for protection of critical information infrastructure in the country.

2. All the data operators or the intermediatory have been mandated to report any cyber security incidents to CERT-In Expeditiously.

3. Cyber Swachhta Kendra (Botnet Cleaning and Malware Analysis Centre) has been launched by the Central Government to enhance the detecting mechanism to detect malicious programmers in the computer devices and provide free tools to remove such corrupt programmers.

4. To form a panel which would issue alert regarding cyber threats and audit the Internet Security Provider services.

5. To conduct regular training session on cyber security and assess the working of Government Organization in safeguarding the interest of users in cyberspace.

6. Conducting regular training programs to make efficiency in working pattern of network system administrators and Chief Information Security Officers (CISOs) of Government and other major Government sectors which work for securing the IT infrastructure and mitigating cyber-attacks in cyber space.

---

[132] Cybercrime and Cybersecurity in India, *available at:* https://www.insightsonindia.com9 (last visited on June 21, 2021)
[133] *Ibid*

7. In order to control the cybercrime cases that takes place against women and children, the Central Government initiated a scheme under the name Cyber Crime Prevention against Women and Children (CCPWC) which establishes an effective infrastructure to handle cybercrimes against women and children in the country. CCPWC is an initiative taken by the Government of India under the National Mission for the safety of women by using the Nirbhaya funds to report cybercrime complaints online when and provide help to those women belonging from marginalized section of society. Under the scheme a portal has been opened by the government to redress the grievances based on complaints relating to Child Pornography, Child Sexual Abuse Material (CSAM) or sexually explicit content such as Rape/Gang Rape (CP/RGR) content which is published online.[134]

8. The Central Government passed the Personal Data Protection Bill ,2018 and revised the same again in 2019 in order to protect the personal data of the users and imposes liability on the government and companies to protect the data of every user and keep all confidential documents and records in secret .It imposes liability on the online intermediator to uphold the confidentiality of its user in every situation and shall not share the same with outsider except to law officer in any investigation carried out in accordance with law.[135]

THE PERSONAL DATA PROTECTION BILL,2019:

Data breach and privacy infringement has become major problem for the internet users. The personal information about the users is being stolen from their accounts and being sold out for profit by the perpetrators. The personal information might be used by the companies, government or any other body and misuse it. The bill laid down provisions thus enabling the data fiduciary to collect all relevant data of the users and preserve it without sharing it with other. In case the user finds that the particular information about him/her is not correct or wish to make any changes in it can ask the data fiduciary to do so. The data fiduciary is under obligation to protect

---

[134] Cybercrime Prevention Against Women and Children (CCPWC) available at: *https://www.journalsofindia.com* (last visited on June 21, 2021).
[135] DATA PROTECTION BILL,2019, available at: *https://www.insightsonline.com* *(last visited on June 22, 2021)*

the personal data of the user and not to process it without prior consent from the user until and unless it is required by the investigating officer during an investigation, or in case of medical emergency. The bill even regulated the transfer of data exchange that takes place across borders by imposing restrictions on the companies to store the personal data of their users only in India and not in other nation. This bill was drafted under chairmanship of Justice (Retd)B. N Shrikrishna with a view of framing such draft which protect the right of privacy of the internet users as the fundamental right guaranteed under constitution and provide data security to every individual while they access online services.[136] The concern over data protection was raised in a case before apex court where the court granted the status of fundamental right to "privacy" and asked the government to frame such policies which protected personal information of the users.[137]

ROLE OF NATIONAL COMMISSION FOR WOMEN

National Commission for Women (NCW) is a statutory body formed under National Commission for Women Act, 1990 whose function is to redress the grievances of the women in our society and work towards their overall socio-economic development. The commission review the policy and legal statute which are framed to protect interest of women and look forward for women empowerment in society. The main aim behind establishing the commission was to sensitize the gender-based discrimination and curb the menace of violence against women to which women are subjected in every part of our country. The National Commission for Women work in the direction to promote welfare of women and assist the government to enact such laws which stop subjugation of women to violence and make them aware about their rights. Today, violence against women in cyberspace is increasing at a greater pace thus injuring the reputation of women in our society. The NCW has taken cyber crime against women into consideration and to address this issue it has formed a redressal mechanism which look into the matter victimization of women cyberspace. It has its own portal where the aggrieved women file a complaint about any cyber crime such as cyber defamation, cyber stalking, sexual exploitation on social media,

---

[136] *Ibid*
[137] *K. PUTTASWAMY vs. UNION OF INDIA. A.I.R 2017*

or any act which resulted into injuring her reputation. The grievance redressal mechanism of NCW on receiving such complaint, establish an inquiry committed which take cognizance of the matter and initiate a legal proceeding with the help of police in investigating the matter.[138] Due to the patriarchal social setup in our nation, women are taught not to speak out if they are victimized in any way, thus, when a women get victimized un cyberspace she finds it difficult to report the same to anyone. Therefore, NCW provides a friendly platform where women can complaint about cyber offence committed against them online without going to police station. It has even made a proposal to Centre Government to enact cyber laws which especially deals only with women and young children rights to curb the menace of cyber offence.

3.10 A WAY FORWARD:

While India has taken a step forward in digitalizing every aspect of day-to-day activity, it is no exception to cyber-attack. In order to combat the menace of data breach and increase in criminal activities which are instituted against women and young children in particular, the Government of India has initiated some steps to regulate the criminal acts which are prevailing in virtual space. The Central Government has made proposal of increasing the age limit of majority from 18 years to 21 to access internet facilities for future generation. The main idea behind it is to eliminate the risk of young children to become victim of cyber attacks as at early age they are not able to understand the nature of offence and consequence resulting out of it. If this proposal get ascent from both houses, then it will be lex loci and its violation will result into penalty.

The passing of Personal Data Protection Bill of 2019 is a cornerstone which has provided protection to individual personal data and has upheld the value of right to privacy in virtual space as enshrined under Indian Constitution. Irrespective of this Bill there still lies some lacunae in our legal system and it needs to be rectified and redrafted according to the changing need of the internet users. Yet, the Government of India has been working hard in the direction of cyber security and scrutinized the

---

[138] *Ibid*

need for a national cyber security system to protect the individual right and avoid cyber warfare in future.

3.11 LACUANE IN OUR PRESENT LEGAL SYSTEM DEALING WITH THE MENACE OF CYBER CRIME AGAINST WOMEN:

Cyber crime is no more a new term added to crime, as the people who are tech-savvy are known to it. But everyone who is having access to internet services might not even be aware about any such crime committed online. In past few years we have witnessed a gradual increase in the number of cyber offences carried in the virtual space which has direct affect on the personal life of the victim. It even poses a great threat to national security as chances of cyber warfare are getting more prevalent. While the main concern about the damage that is bound to rise out of cyber offences.

The Government of India realized this and to curb the menace of cyber crimes enacted the Information Technology Act, 2000 which defines the term cybercrime and prescribe punishment for the same. But when it comes to eliminating the cyber violence against women the present statute seems to be quite on it. Moreover, the Information Technology was particularly enacted to regulate the online transaction and e-commerce business. Even at present the provisions of IT Act, 2000 are taken into consideration while deciding any fraudulent transaction or money laundering cases. Although, the Information Technology (Amendment) Act of 2008 added certain provision into the act which covered certain malicious act carried online such as cyber defamation, child pornography, publication of indecent material concerning child etc. and penalized the culprit invading privacy of the users. But irrespective of adding new provision in IT Act concerning individual rights, there seems no end in criminal activities committed against women in cyber space. Some of the main reason for failure of IT Act in curbing cyber menace are as follow:

- **JURISDICTION ASSPECT IN CYBERSPACE:**

While initiating proceeding under criminal or civil law jurisdiction to try the case is an important part of Judicial System. The court try any case if it has jurisdiction over it. To try any case in court of law jurisdiction of court matters and includes namely- Personal Jurisdiction, Territorial Jurisdiction, and Pecuniary Jurisdiction. Based on these jurisdictions the court take cognizance of a case and initiate further proceeding. In case of cybercrime which takes place in cyber space the jurisdiction to try the matter depends on three main type of jurisdiction that are:[139]

1. PERSPECTIVE JURISDICTION:

Perspective Jurisdiction is a jurisdiction that is responsible for the proceedings against the accused by the state for infringing the rights of others guaranteed by the constitution.

2. JURISDICTION TO ADJUDICATE:

Jurisdiction to adjudicate generally refers to power of a state to bring a person to a court or any tribunal whether civil or criminal where proceedings are carried out, state may be may not be party to the case. In such cases a relationship is there between the state and the person concerned.

3. Jurisdiction to Enforce: Jurisdiction to enforce empowers the state to penalize the person for his wrongdoings and non-compliance with the law of the land. The laws of the state are enforced by the legal officers, in compliance with prior permission of the concerned state authority.

While deciding case of cybercrime the abovementioned jurisdiction is taken care of by the court of law. The Budapest Convention gives a brief account on the jurisdictional right of trying the offender from any part of the world by those nation where cyber crime is instituted and those who are member state to the convention.

While India not being a part of the Budapest Convention lack the power to adjudicate any person belonging to other nation in accordance to the laws prevailing in India. Cyber crime can take place anywhere and in nay form. The perpetrator may commit crime from any part of the world, therefore, making it difficult for the states to

---

[139] Cyberspace Jurisdiction: Issues and Challenges, *available at: https:// www.legalbites* .in (last visited on June 22, 2021)

adjudicate the case and enforce the law of land on such person. Without having jurisdiction to try a case, it become difficult to hold the criminals accountable for their malicious acts Thus, this situation gives an opportunity to the offender to escape the legal proceeding and indulges into other criminal acts. This has further aggravated the instances of cyber crime against women as it gives an easy hand to the perpetrator to exploit the victim more often.

Unlike European Nations, where they have special laws which restrict the companies from using any personal data of users and laws especially dealing with cyber offences committed against women and young children, in India we only have one cyber law which deals more in commercial transactions in particular then in online criminal acts. India being a diversified nation need more outward and enhanced cyber law which take into consideration the cultural aspect of our society and lay such efficient guidelines which not only help to curb the menace of cyber crimes against women but even make them aware about their rights.

Moreover, to combat the menace of cybercrime India need to become a state party to the Budapest Convention and work towards amending its cyber laws in more comprehensive manner so that it covers every crime that is meted out on women and young children. The Indian Criminal System is also full of lacunae when it comes to addressing the grievances of women in general. It has been seen that the criminal law is more or less friendly while dealing cases where man is a victim. Whereas the criminal legal system is less sensitive towards victimization of women. Irrespective of having so many provisions laid down under Indian Criminal Law which protects the women against cruelty and violence, the women are seen less as victim and more as a reason for crime in our society.

The police and other officials do not take the issues of women victimization so seriously and instead of doing their duty they tend to act as a negotiator between the criminal and victim, thus making it easy for culprit to harass the women in future. Therefore, it becomes crucial for the government as well to establish special police officer team which are well educated and aware about the cybercrime and their impact on the personal and social life of the victim.

ROLE OF JUDICIARY

CHAPATER 4

4.1 ROLE OF JUDICIARY IN COMABTIMG CRIME AGAINST WOMEN

Technology has played an important role in our life from the time when we used to communicate through telegrams and other postal services, until today where we have internet and social media sites to interact with our family and friends. With an easy access to internet services, it not just connected whole world on one single platform but also imparted socio-cultural awareness among masses hailing from various other nations. But certainly, with all its positive shades lies the darkest side also and has strongly affected our daily life. With all its benefits it has also brought a new phenomenon of cybercrime into being. In 21st century Cybercrime has emerged as new and complex type of crimes which has posed a challenge to our legislation in order to curb its menace and protect the rights of the users. it.

Crime rate in India is already high at an alarming rate and to add more to it cybercrimes are contributing more ten ever before. It gets more challenging to curb the menace of cybercrime in India due to lack of awareness among masses due to the poor legal infrastructure and lack of understanding among masses about the online offences. Due to patriarchal setup and pre dominance of male section in our society make women vulnerable to become a victim of gender-based violence even in the virtual sphere. Online gender-based violence includes crimes such as; Cyber harassment, Cyber stalking, Cyber pornography, Cyber bullying based on sexual orientation, Cyber defamation, Morphing, Email Spoofing, publishing of indecent images of women online, etc. have been increasing due to digital revolution.

In this era of digital world women and young children are being targeted beneath the curtain of cyber space and are easy to be victimized without coming into light. With the changing nature of crime and its impact on social order make it evident for the adjudicating authority to take the matter of cyber offence into consideration and provide a just and fair society for every individual without any gender discrimination.

As on today with the misuse of Information Arachnology the criminals' acts leads to unrest in our society. Therefore, to combat this situation an appropriate approach of judiciary is required to curb and prevent further crimes.[140]

The judiciary has always played a major role whenever the crime has taken over the social order. Judiciary is regarded as the guardian or our democratic for the very reason that it protects the interest of every individual by making a society free from crime and violence. The Indian Judiciary has always taken into consideration the rights of the individual and passed such judgements which changed the whole outlook of our legal system. For proper and efficient working of the judiciary it becomes important that it holds jurisdiction over particular matter. To protect the interest of every person there is a need for effective legal mechanism which lays down rules and regulation which serves the purpose of transparency and efficient judicial role. At present the judiciary has been actively participating in the policies which are framed for women empowerment. The judiciary takes the cognizance of the violence that is meted out on the women in particular in the cyberspace. The court of law has rendered some important judgements, whereby they protected the interest of women in cyber space and make same a safe platform to which a woman has access without nay threat of apprehension of fear.

In every democratic system judiciary plays a pivotal role in ascertaining the human rights of its citizens and preserving the sanctity of constitution. Judiciary is an independent wing of the government, which interpret the laws in force and resolve dispute between partis and deliver

---

[140] Ibid

justice to the victim. In order to have a peaceful and well-developed society we require a powerful and transparent adjudicating authority which owes its duty to protect the society from all social evils, and judiciary is the one who protect our rights and promote humanity. The society is ever changing, and at present technology has brought a drastic change in our social setup. It has paved a new way for criminals to commit crime. With the emergence of cybercrime and its repercussion in society and the victim behavior, poses a challenge for judiciary to prevent the menace of cybercrime. In past few years we have witnessed a gradual surge in the incidence of cyber violence carried out against women in cyber space. The judiciary has played a significant role in delivering justice to the victimized women and setting precedent for future cases as well. Some landmark judgements which represent the role of judiciary in fighting against cybercrime against women are as follow:

- **RITU KOHLI CASE STUDY**

It was the first reported case of cyber stalking in India. It was for the first time that a new word was coined by the court of law naming it as Cyber Stalking. Usually, we have heard about stalking in general where the offender monitors every activity of the victim and note it down and in future abet a crime against them. But in this case a women named Ritu Kohli who was married was stalked online. In this case the main issue which was raised in front of the court was what is cyber stalking and why we have no proper legislation to punish the offender for same. In present case the offender named Manish used to stalk the victim and used her identity to make a fake account on other site and used to chat with other people with her name using obnoxious language and posting obscene content online and made regular call on her number. The culprit posted her number online, and after this she used to get unwanted calls from different people constantly from different parts of world. She filed a complaint in the Delhi Police station and the officer there lodged an F.I.R under section 509 of IPC.

The question before the court was that section 509 does not cover acts committed online. The court asked the government to look into such matters of crime that are carried out in cyber space. The court ruled that without any adequate law it seems difficult to address the issue and penalize the offender without proper criminal law. Thus, it was after this case that section 66A was added to Information Technology

(Amendment) Act,2008 which laid down provisions in relation to cyber stalking and prescribed punishment for the same.[141]

- **SUHAS KATTI CASE**

This was the first case, whereby the offender was convicted under the Information Technology Act, 2000 for committing cyber offence by the court. This case generally falls under the category of publishing or transmitting indecent and obscene material online. In this particular case the offender was a good friend of the victim and wished to marry her, but the victim turned down his proposal and married someone else. Later on, the victim got separated from her husband and divorced him. On finding that the victim was single, the offender again with the same intention tried to pursued her, but she had no consensus over this and rejected his proposal. This ultimately provoked the offender who was a snubbed suitor and to satiate his vengeance he made a fake account of her and posted her images with indecent captions with an aim to harass her. He posted her images to defame her and malign her character in the society. After this she received number of emails from various number, who thought her to be a prostitute and asked about her business and cost relating to it. Later on, she lodged an F.I.R against Suhas who was the main culprit behind the curtains and he was charged under section 469, 509 of Indian Penal Code and section 67 of Information Technology Act, 2000. The court ruled out that outraging the modesty of women either by gesture, words or by publishing such content online against women which bring disrepute to her character and injures her reputation is a criminal act and the offender doing so shall be punished with rigorous imprisonment in order to have a deter effect on others also.[142]

- **THE DELHI PUBLIC SCHOOL CASE**

---

[141] *Ritu Kohli vs. Manish Kathuria* A.I.R 2001
[142] *SUHAS KATTI vs. STATE OF TAMIL NADU*, A.I.R 2004

The Delhi Public School case also known by DPS sex scandal, was the case which raised an alarm regarding child pornography. In the particular case a video of a girl from DPS school while intimating with her friend was video filmed by the culprit and was published online in a form of mms of 2 mi. In this case the CEO Avinash was arrested for providing internet service to his user to publish such sexual content online.

The video got circulated through out India within 24 hours of posting. The young girl was bullied and harassed by the society for her such conduct. The court took cognizance of the case and held Avinash liable for such publication and arrested him under section 67 of Information Technology Act, 2000. After this case the court ordered the government to formulate certain guidelines to make the service provider liable for making his computer resource available to carry any cybercrime against the user, women and young girls in particular. The government of India took up the matter and Intermediatory guidelines and rules were passed in the year 2011, under which duty was imposed on the intermediator or internet service provider to protect the sensible data of the user and in case he shares any personal content with outsider he shall be liable for it and be penalized in accordance to with the provisions of Information Technology Act, 2000. Their liability will only absolve if they paid due diligence in preserving the personal data of the user to assure no obscene content is published or transmitted through their computer resources.[143]

- **T.S BALAN AND ANEESH BALAN CASE:**

It was the first case in which e-court played a significant role in combating the growing trend of cyber crime against women. The case was filed against the priest and his father by their partner. In a skirmish between the two parties the priest and the son committed cybercrime and was held guilty for morphing, web-hosting and sending e-mailing nude of his sister and family to bring disrepute to the family members in society. The accused posted morphed images of family member on the web page to take revenge. In this case the police took all computer used for

---

[143] *Avinash Bajaj vs. State of Delhi, A.I.R 2008*

publishing such content into their custody and hired a computer analyst to gather all evidence. It was the first case in which the local court passed out punishment in a cyber-attack case and the e- discovery was given an upper hand while conducting investigation.[144]

- ## Dr. L. PRAKASH VS STATE OF TAMIL NADU

This case gained attention as being a high-profile case of cyber pornography case which was committed by a doctor. The orthopedic doctor named L. Prakash used to seek sexual favor from his women patient and his assistance would do videography of all the intimacy moments and without their knowledge and later on sent the whole video to his brother living abroad, who used to post the same on various porn sites and get monetary benefit out of it. Later on, one relative of victim came across a clipping where the women who was in unconscious state was being involved in intimacy scene with the doctor and whole moment was video graphed and was getting viral online. Then the matter was reported to the Tamil Nadu police and case was initiated in the court. He was charged under section 67 of Information Technology Act, 2000 and sent behind prison for a term of 10 years for abducting women and forcing them into pornography racket. He was even booked under Indecent Representation of Women Act, for kidnapping women and sexually exploiting them and engaged in erotica business.[145] Although it was the first case of cybercrime which came up into public just within one year of passing the IT Act ,2000.

- ## SADDAM HUSSAIN: CYBER BLACKMAILING CASE

The present case deals with cyber exploitation of the victim by sexually exploiting her and later on blackmailed her. The offender Saddam Hussain sexually abused a woman and recorded the same. He used to threaten the victim by blackmailing her on bases of publishing and sharing the recorder video of her online. By blackmailing her

---

[144] *Balan vs. State of Kerala, A.I.R 2003*, 436
[145] *Dr. L Prakash vs. State of Tamil Nadu* ,2002

he used to take sexual favor from her and forced her to indulge in sexual activities. The victim was sexually and mentally assaulted by the offender every now and then. Later on the victim lodged an F.I.R against the offender and case was instituted against him in court. Court took the cognizance of the case and punished the offender relevant provisions of IT Act ,2000 and IPC of 1860.[146]

- **SHREYA SINGHAL CASE STUDY**

It was one of the landmark cases, whereby the Apex Court invalidated Section 66A of Information Technology Act, 2000. The validity of the said section was challenged on the ground that it was against the provisions of Article 19(2) of Indian Constitution. A petition was forwarded before the Supreme Court of Indi a, by which the petitioner contented that the language of Section 66A was quite vague and annoying and violated their right to speech and expression to which they are entitled under Article 19. The language of 66A was vague as it prohibited publishing of any information online or through any electronic medium which was injurious for society. But the language was not clear in its sense about which content falls under the section and which doesn't fit within the section. Everything was just based on one's apprehension, therefore obstructing the user even from giving his opinion on some content.

In this case 2 women were arrested for posting offensive comments on fakebook over shutting down of whole city of Mumbai on the death ceremony of a political leader. The police made arrest under section 66 of Information Technology Act, 2000 whereby anyone who transmit any information through computer source which is offensive, or such information is made to create unrest or annoyance in society. Although later on both of the accused ladies were released as the arrest was made in hastily manner. The women then filed a petition before the Apex court, challenging the constitutional validity of Section 66A of IT Act ,2000.

---

[146] *Saddam Hussain vs. State of M.P* (2016) SCC MP 1411

The court took up the matter and found that the language enunciated under aforementioned section was vague and ambiguous as by virtue of it one can't even express his views and opinions on any matter which might be of public concern, thus, violating the fundamental right of an individual under Article 19(2). It was then that the court held section 66A as unconstitutional and invalidated the same.[147]

- On an PIL filled by one NGO named Prajwala, which brought the matter of sexual exploitation of women and young children on social media sites in form of child pornography, sexual exploitation of women, defaming, bullying them, and trafficking of women for flesh trade, gang rape videos was getting more prominent, and no check was there on it. The Hon'ble Supreme Court took cognizance of the matter and sou moto the central government to look into this matter where online crime against women and children was mercilessly carried through various social media platforms, and directed the government to form such online portal to which the victim has easy access and can lodge complaint about any cybercrime that takes place against them. Further, the Apex court also sought a reply from the parties before it -Yahoo, Facebook, Google India Inc, Microsoft and WhatsApp, on the recommendations made by the Ajith Kumar Committee and the policies framed by these social media sites to curb the menace of sexual exploitation that is getting very common on their sites and what are the measures taken by them to eliminate it. But these companies did not comply with the order to Supreme court and therefore they were slammed a fine of 1,00,000 (Rupees One Lakh) for not following the directions of the court.

The Apex court has been taking the matter of sexual violence and trafficking of women and young children into consideration and has asked the state as well as the Central Government to frame such policies to eliminate the ever-growing threat of cybercrime against women.

- **PUBLISHING OBSCENE MATERIAL**

---

[147] Shreya Singhal vs. Union of India, A.I.R 2015 SC 1523

The concept of revenge porn came into light in a case in which a snubbed suitor in order to take revenge from the victim with whom he was in a relationship. The offender video graphed the intimate moments with the victim when they were in good terms with each other. Later on, when the victim refused to marry the offender, he deliberately blackmailed her by sending all indecent images of her, and then he published all images and video of the victim in a compromising situation online. This was the first reported case of revenge porn, where the offender to take revenge from the victim published obscene content online describing her in order to bring disrepute to her image in society.

The Hight Court of West Bengal ordered conviction of the offender under section 66E,66C ,67, 66A of Information Act of 2000 and Section 354, 354A, 354C and 509 of Indian Penal Code.[148]

- **PRIYA DARSHINI MATO CASE:**

This case was a planned cold murder case. In the present case victim Priya Darshini who was a 25-year-old law student was brutally raped and murdered by the offender, Santosh Kumar, who was the son of Inspector General of Police. The victim and the accused were pursuing their carrier in law from Delhi University. It was from that time the accused used to harass, assault and stalked her. The victim used to get calls from the accessed and used to harass her. The victim lodged F.I.R against him twice and even informed the dean of their department about the malicious activities of the offender. Irrespective of filing lodging complaint no action was brought on serious note against the offender as he had an influential family background. The case took new phase with the brutal killing of the victim by the offender. During investigation it was found that the victim was raped by the offender and then brutally killed her by hitting her with his helmet and then strangulated her to a fan in her room to give it a color of suicide. The lower court awarded death penalty to the accused. While later on the offender appealed the Apex Court for his acquittal, the court after examining the case commuted death penalty into life imprisonment. In this case there was tampering with the evidences and the witnesses were also threatened by the police.

---

[148] State of West Bengal vs. Animesh Boxi, GR:1587/17

Many questions were raised over the role of judiciary and the police, as their duty is to safeguard interest of ever individual and not of only those who belong from well to do families. The judiciary took up this matter and directed the police department that saving interest of one person in present case was unjust and give opportunity to other to commit gender-based offences. The court asked the government to frame policies to protect the interest of women in our society and make provisions for their empowerment.[149]

RIGHT TO PRIVACY

In 2017 the Supreme Court verdict on right to privacy as a fundamental right changed the whole concept of confidentiality in real and virtual world. Usually known by the name Aadhar case, gained lot of attention as earlier there was no provision which protected privacy of individual. A nine-judge bench of the Hon'ble Supreme Court in K. Puttaswamy case passed a judgement securing the personal liberty as an inseparable part of right to liberty and declared right to privacy as a fundamental right. The state and non- state parties are bound by it and only under some reasonable restrictions the right to privacy can be revoked by state. This judgement has several implications by which right to privacy scope has been widened up and includes;

1. The right to privacy expressly recognizes an individual free will to choose his /her sexual orientation without any interference from the state or other person.
2. One of the important aspects of passing this judgement can be seen in terms of using internet services. By virtue of this right every internet user has right to privacy in cyberspace as well.
3. The court imposes duty over state and private companies to formulate such policies in order to regulate the privacy policy and data protection of every user. Court laid emphases on data protection and asked the government to frame such policies to protect personal data of the user and avoid any crime online against them. It was in reference to this case that Personal Data Protection Bill was

---

[149] A.I.R 1996

passed in 2019 to impose liability on the intermediatory to protect personal information of every subscriber.
4. With imposing liability on intermediaries and private companies for protecting data of the subscriber made it easy for the court to hold accountability of them in case any offence occurs on their computer resources and avoid cybercrime.

The initiative taken by Judiciary of granting status of fundamental right to privacy in real and virtual world has brought a revolutionary change by granting every individual a liberty to choose their sexual orientation, protect every personal credential from being misused by the authorities or the companies.

4.2 CHALLENGES FACED BY JUDICIARY IN CYBERSPACE

The Indian Judiciary has always played a crucial role in establishing such society where a free and fair environment is provided for every citizen for their personal and social growth by removing all evil practices from society. With an aim to maintain sanctity of justice, it tries to eliminate all sorts of malpractices which tend to corrupt the society and hamper the peace in society. In same way it has tried through its various judgement to protect the female section of our society against violence in the virtual space. Although, it has set out certain precedent by protecting interest of women in cyberspace, yet it faces certain challenges to eliminate the evils of cybercrime from penetrating into society and attacking female section of society. Thus, the challenges faced by judiciary generally includes:[150]

1. JURISDICTIONAL ISSUE:

Jurisdiction issue is the major problem for the judiciary while adjudicating upon the cases of cyber offences. The cyber space is vast in its dimension and the criminal

---

[150] A Challenging Role of Indian Judiciary In Cyberspace, *available at :* https://www.gapinterdisciplinarities.org (last visited on June 23, 2021)

may attack the victim from any part of the world and this leads to jurisdictional issue. If a cybercrime is committed within the Indian Territory, then it gets easy for the court to apply territorial jurisdiction in such cases and adjudicate upon the matter, but where the criminal is sitting overseas, the question of jurisdiction arises as the court can't exercise its power in such cases. Thus, resulting into delay in justice.

2. TRADITIONAL WAY OF CONDUCTING INVESTIGATION:

Another feature which challenges role of judiciary is the old ways of carrying out investigation. In India even today the way of carrying investigation is old and delaying in nature. It takes months to investigate the following matter in concern. Even after so much development in ITC field, its usage in investigation is not seen. If the investigation agency uses ITC in conducting investigation it would be easy and time saving for both -the agency and the judiciary.

3. CHALLENGE IN COLLECTING DIGITAL EVIDENCE:

With so much data available online, it really becomes difficult for the investigating agencies to collect relevant evidence. As multifarious devices are used by the perpetrator in order to commit cyber offence, it becomes difficult for the investigating agencies to collect relevant evidences from these resources and thus, question of their legality arises in the court.

4. INAAPPROPRIATE LEGAL PROVISONS:

The main duty of judiciary is to interpret law in its best sense to suit all citizens need. But it becomes difficult for the judiciary to interpret laws if they are inappropriate and vague in its nature. While we talk about IT Act,2000 provisions which protect interest of women in cyberspace, it is not properly given itself in the act which section deals with women protection in virtual world and this creates a chaos, whereby making it difficult for the judiciary to comprehend the law and penalize the offender.[151]

5. LACK OF AWRAENESS ABOUT TECHNOLOGY AMONG OFFICIALS:

Another issue which stipulates the challenges faced by judiciary in deciding a cybercrime case is due to lack of knowledge about the usage of technology among investigating officials. The officials generally lack the knowledge about the operation of new software and other technological advancement which has occurred in past few years, thus making the investigation machinery unreliable. Due to lack of knowledge among officials about recent technological advancement, it becomes difficult for the court to fully rely on the report submitted by agencies as it is full of lacunae in it and this might result in unfair delivery of justice.

6. LACK OF SKILLED HUMAN RESOURCE IN LEGAL SYSTEM:

In order to have fast and fair trial in court, it becomes necessary to have well-equipped and skilled human labor who have vast knowledge about cyber space. In our criminal legal system, we need efficient and well learned experts, who deals especially in the matter of ITC department and help the judiciary to have better understanding about its features and how it is used to carry out malpractices in general. But due to unavailability of such cyber expert it becomes difficult for the judiciary to understand the features of new technology and the mens rea of particular act committed in cyber space. Moreover, unlike foreign nations we do not have separate cybercells to deal only in cybercrimes. This causes delay in justice as the Indian judiciary is already burdened due to pilling of cases. Therefore, it is important to have cyber cells with well versed cyber experts who posse's knowledge about cyberspace and help in disposing of cases ion time in fair manner. There is a need to establish fast track courts which have adjudicating power in cases of cybercrime, this would eventually speed up the trial and avoid overburden of cases on court. These cyber cells shall be construed in such a way that it consists of judges or legal experts

---

[151] *Ibid*

who are well versed with the new technology and have in depth knowledge about the scientific approach which could be applied while deciding a particular case.

7: AMBIGUITY IN THE CYBER LAWS

The language of the Information Technology Act, 2000, is not clear when it comes to ascertaining the rights of users against violence in cyberspace. While dealing in case where women is victimized in cyber world, the cyber laws enacted does not provide a detailed account on when a women rights is violated. It defines cybercrime as a whole, but does not make provisions which exclusively deals with crime against women. Thus, making it difficult for the judges to interpret its language and deliver justice.

8.LACK OF SCEURITY TOOLS

Lack of security tools creates a massive problem of collecting evidences and presenting it before the court of law. Due to this, sometimes the evidence brought in the court might cause doubt over the efficacy of our criminal procedural law and make it difficult for the judges to deliver justice.

Irrespective of the flaws that are present in our legal system, the judiciary has always provided a homage to the one whose rights are violated. Judiciary has always worked in a positive direction by serving its utmost gratitude towards individual rights in the virtual space. Thus, without an independent judiciary it becomes difficult to uphold the integrity and sovereignty of a democratic nation. The heart of democracy lies in its judiciary system as it provides shelter to every citizen irrespective of any discrimination by preserving their rights and privileges. The Indian Judiciary act as a guiding light for the government while framing any policies as it keeps in few that the ultimate goal behind framing any bill or laws is to establish a fair and just society for all living being. Even in case of cyber crimes judiciary has never stepped back, instead it has made proposal to the government to frame such rules and regulations which ultimately aims at protecting the interest of women and young children in the dark web.

CYBERCRIMES AGAINST WOMEN – A QUANTITATIVE PICTURE

CHAPTER 5

In India, cybercrime against women year by year is showing an upward trend as is illustrated in the listed account or data provided by NCRB for the years 2017 and 2018. State and Union Territories wise segmentation of cybercrime helps to deduce a distinctive inference regarding cybercrimes.

It is also to be noted that the data enlisted under is only taking account of reported incidents and reality may be in stark juxtaposition to what the conclusions it seems to give at first sight. [152]

---

[152] Cybercrime against women In India, *available at :* https://ncrb.gov.in (last visited on June 23, 2021)

The increasing data trend published by NCRB is due to numerous reasons, couple of them are enumerated below as –

1.) Easy Accessibility of Internet
2.) Sense of Anonymity
3.) Lack of strict regulations
4.) Advanced Hacking Tools
5.) Easy access to personal information of users on networking sites
6.) Internet being a pertinent tool to circulate information by the speed of light
7.) Personal Motivations–
    a.) Defamation
    b.) Vengeance
    c.) Frauds relating to monetary affairs
    d.) Online Grooming

These are just some of the reasons which have contributed to the rise of cybercrime, there are many other corrupt mindsets as well which inspires such crimes to happen in our society and victims can never understand what the criminal is scheming in the absence of their awareness.

The present report submitted herein, provides detailed account of sexual harassment of women in cyberspace.

The inference which is to be drawn from the mentioned data gives a brief insight how internet related crimes has penetrated deep into our system and disturbing the social order in terms of causing unrest in society.

Moreover, the gender -based discrimination in the cyberspace has led to victimization of women to a great extent and the most common cyber offences to which women are subjected are generally sexual offences which injures the dignity of women in society.

States	Cyber Pornography/ Hosting/Publishing Obscene Sexual Materials		Cyber Stalking, Cyber Bullying of Women		Other Crimes against Women		Total Cyber Crimes against Women		Total Cyber Crimes in the State/UT		%	
	2017	2018	2017	2018	2017	2018	2017	2018	2017	2018	2017	2018
Andhra Pradesh	1	5	48	82	110	96	173	217	931	1207	18.58%	17.97%
Arunachal Pradesh#	0	0	0	0	0	1	0	1	1	7	N.A.	14.28%
Assam#	76	172	12	18	198	357	379	670	1120	2022	33.83%	33.13%
Bihar	4	2	2	2	30	6	36	14	433	374	8.31%	3.74%
Chhattisgarh	1	15	11	14	73	33	89	64	171	139	52.04%	46.04%
Goa	0	3	0	0	9	18	9	21	13	29	69.23%	72.41%
Gujarat	3	11	15	11	69	151	94	184	458	702	20.52%	26.21%
Haryana	6	34	27	5	36	64	79	112	504	418	15.67%	26.79%
Himachal Pradesh	6	27	1	1	9	18	30	52	56	69	53.57%	75.36%
Jammu & Kashmir	2	6	1	0	8	10	13	23	63	73	20.63%	31.50%
Jharkhand	0	8	2	0	24	5	26	13	720	930	3.61%	1.39%
Karnataka	24	42	14	4	681	1322	729	1374	3174	5839	22.96%	23.53%
Kerala	10	53	8	8	96	84	126	160	320	340	39.37%	47.05%
Madhya Pradesh	21	52	25	36	145	183	192	276	490	740	39.18%	37.29%
Maharashtra	14	31	301	398	787	815	1119	1262	3604	3511	31.04%	35.94%
Manipur	0	1	7	3	19	5	27	9	74	29	36.48%	31.03%
Meghalaya#	2	1	0	0	3	28	6	32	39	74	15.38%	43.24%
Mizoram	0	0	0	0	3	4	4	4	10	6	40%	66.66%
Nagaland	0	0	0	0	0	1	0	2	0	2	N.A.	100%
Odisha	23	172	6	7	33	13	62	228	824	843	7.52%	27.04%
Punjab	3	26	7	16	41	44	61	97	176	239	34.65%	40.58%
Rajasthan	5	10	12	30	67	59	89	116	1304	1104	6.82%	10.50%
Sikkim#	0	1	0	0	0	0	0	1	1	1	N.A.	100%

State	C1	C2	C3	C4	C5	C6	C7	C8	C9	C10	C11	C12
Tamil Nadu	8	26	2	1	24	47	53	77	228	295	23.24%	26.10%
Telangana	24	42	27	18	130	254	196	336	1209	1205	16.21%	27.88%
Tripura	0	4	0	0	1	0	1	5	7	20	14.28%	25%
Uttar Pradesh	17	91	6	24	231	217	265	340	4971	6280	5.33%	5.41%
Uttarakhand	2	10	0	9	10	35	30	78	124	171	24.19%	45.61%
West Bengal#	4	2	9	18	201	139	270	170	568	335	47.53%	50.74%
Total State(s)	256	847	543	705	3038	4009	4158	5938	21,593	27,004	19.25%	21.98%
Union Territory.												
Andaman & Nicobar Islands	0	1	0	0	2	4	2	5	3	7	66.66%	71.42%
Chandigarh	2	0	2	5	0	0	5	5	32	30	15.62%	16.66%
Dadra & N.A. Nagar Haveli	0	0	1	0	0	0	1	0	1	0	100%	N.A.
Daman & Diu	0	0	0	0	0	0	0	0	0	0	N.A.	N.A.
Delhi	13	13	9	28	47	33	76	79	162	189	46.91%	41.79%
Lakshadweep	0	1	0	0	0	2	0	3	0	4	N.A.	75%
Puducherry	0	0	0	0	0	0	0	0	5	14	N.A.	N.A.
Total UT(s)	15	15	12	33	49	39	84	92	203	244	41.37%	37.70%
Total All India	271	862	555	738	3087	4048	4242	6030	21,796	27,248	19.46%	22.13%

Data released by NCRB mentioned above gives the account of cybercrimes that took place in 2017 and 2018. According to the same report, Uttar Pradesh saw the highest number of crimes on cyberspace. Following Uttar Pradesh were the states like Maharashtra, Assam and Karnataka. Thus, it is clearly decipherable from the given data report that what states are leading in the cyber crime cases and which ones are doing best to reduce the number. The given report is thus a marker of state of cybercrimes in India and what are the states and Union Territories which are countering such numbers and which are just staying ignorant of the cybercrimes in their territory. All in all, it can be summed up that the states which are having large population and less regulations regarding cyber space were found much at risk of victimizing the users on internet. Also, victimization of women in states having stereotypical patriarchal setup like Uttar Pradesh and Rajasthan were high in the number of cybercrime cases. Therefore, it is learned that the listed factors contribute in any region to the increase in cybercrimes against women-

1.) Patriarchal bent of mind of citizens in the given region
2.) Lack of awareness of regulations controlling cyberspace
3.) Cyber attack motivated with personal vendetta
4.) Improper implementation of Cyber Laws
5.) Socio cultural factors

Henceforth, cybercrimes in India especially in the states with having male dominant setup were found to have increased incidence rate of cybercrimes than compared to the states extremely opposite in the setup with having men and women sharing equal liberties. Diversity of India is also one point to consider as well to reach at the reason behind the non-uniform cybercrime rate in India as in some areas there are aware citizens who know their rights and regulations regarding cybercrimes and also there are some other regions which are extremely opposite in citizens composition who even lack basic education.

CONCLUSION AND SUGGESTIONS

CHAPTER 6

Crime is an act which is committed against an individual, a state or a community as a whole with a malicious intent to inflict pain and cause harm to them. The concept of crime is not new to us, it has been there in our society since time immemorial. Even in earlier times there used be criminal acts committed with a malicious intent. Looking back at the historical account the ruler used to inflict harsh penalties on the offender who breached the rules or tried to commit offence of treason against the state. The culprit used to be punished only for offences which were committed against state, it was in later period that the act of injuring an individual was recognized and was considered as a criminal offence. Crime exists in every society around the globe, no country is immune from the crime be it a developed nation or developing nations all are affected by crime in general.

While crime is there in our society from the very beginning of human civilization, but it has evolved with every passing phase. The conventional crimes such as murder, extortion, drug trafficking, sexual exploitation of women, human trafficking, terrorism, fraud, money laundering etc. are there from a long time in our society. It is not just confined to a territory or place, but crime can be comfited anywhere at any time. Crime is not limited to a state or person it has a wide range and covers transnational organized crimes which are committed at international level. Like human civilization it has also evolved from old conventional crimes to modern crimes. in 21st century the most prominent crimes that are taking place around the globe are the cyber offences. The shift of conventional crimes to cybercrimes has certainly caused unrest around the globe.

The advancement in the Information Technology brought revolutionary change in the society. The most renowned invention of mankind in the history was the birth of Internet services. INTERNET with its invention in this century is seen as an era from where technological advancement is demarcated as pre and post internet age. Looking back at the time when it was invented no would have ever thought that one day it will become an important facet of our daily requirements.

Internet has become a platform of communication, where people have easy access to communicate with others irrespective of geographical barriers. It serves as a huge platform where not only one can communicate with their loved ones who lives overseas but even provides any sort of information just at a click. Internet has totally changed our lifestyle as everything is available in online mode and you are just a click away from getting any information, to do window shopping, or carry out any business transactions and even online studies has become a trend. It has removed all the socio-cultural barriers that existed prior to coming up to internet. It was considered as the beginning of new era where people from all walks of life would come together and all barriers and prejudices that existed in our society would completely vanish. And today internet has achieved its mission to some extent. However, as coin has two side same is the case with internet, on one hand it served all the purpose of mankind and brought the world together at one platform but on the opposite end it gave birth to online crime.

The internet and social media sites made a room for the notorious elements in our society to carry out criminal activities against the internet users. Online crimes have gained momentum in present time, leaving behind its mark on the one who is victimized in the cyberspace. The cyberspace has turned into a dark sphere where immoral activities are stimulated without any check. To everyone surprise the most targeted group in cyberspace is the female section of our society. The victimization of women in cyber space has increased many folds.

In our society women are always seen as a soft target to be easily assaulted and victimized by the offender. By looking at the present scenario, it can be asserted that violence against women is rising at an alarming rate. Violence against women (VAW) which is peculiarly known as gender-based violence and sexual and gender-based violence (SGBV) are considered those acts which are violent in nature and exclusively committed against women or girls. These offences are gender- based and the offender usually target the vulnerable section of society especially women and girls in any forms. The VAW has a vast history, it is as old as the society itself and the intensity of such violence vary from time to time between societies. Since ancient period, women have always been subjected to all sorts of violence in comparison to the male section of society. The reason behind such violence in literal sense generally arises from the sense of entitlement, male predominance in the society, superiority complex, or the socio-cultural aspect of patriarchal setup. The notion that "women is slave to men and not an equal of men" is still practiced in our society today and they are subjected to violence and cruelty. This notion of subjugation of women in our society gives an opportunity to the offender to further harass the victim.

Violence against women can fit into several broad categories and it includes sexual offences as rape, sexual harassment, domestic violence, acid attacks, reproductive coercion, female infanticide, prenatal sex selection, obstetric violence, as well as there are some customary or traditional practices such as honour killings, dowry violence, female genital mutilation and forced marriage by abduction. To worsen the condition of women in society cybercrime has a significant contribution. The main aim behind targeting women and young girls in cyberspace is to harass them and sexually abuse them for their own sexual gratification or for monetary benefits. The common types of malicious practiced carried in cyberspace against women includes: cyber stalking, cyber defamation, bullying, trolling, making pornography of women, cyber voyeurism, online grooming, privacy infringement, cyber trafficking of women and force them into flesh trade or escort services, etc are carried out in the dark web having a long-lasting impact on the victimized women.

Violence committed against women impacts her overall personal growth, which goes unnoticed in our society due to patriarchal setup and male dominance in society. The plight of women in cyberspace usually goes unnoticed due to lack of awareness about the cybercrime and their rights against sexual exploitation in virtual world. Most of the women are unaware about their rights and are afraid to speak out loud about the violation committed against them due to our social setup where women have no say even in family matters. This situation leads to agender- biased community where the women will be treated next to cattle and her freedom to speech is snatched by the male dominating society and making her vulnerable to be victimized frequently ever now and then.

In order to stop this overhauling prejudice of forming a gender -biased society where women are always subjected to violence, a strong legal framework is required. In India, the victimization of women and young girls due to their gender has always been a matter of concern for the law enforcing agencies. In order to combat crime, it becomes evident that firstly we remove all age-old norms and prejudices established by our community, where discrimination has always been there to hamper over all growth of individual and society as a whole. The Indian Constitution and Criminal Justice System has worked in the direction of protecting the female section of our society from getting sexually exploited in the real and the virtual world. The Government of India has passed some statutes which particularly deals with protection of women against any violent act which cause grave injury to her dignity in society.

LEGAL FRAMEWORK ENLISTED TO CURB MENACE OF CYBER CRIME AGAINST WOMEN:

In today's techno-savvy environment, the world is getting more advanced and digitally sophisticated. This has widened the scope of cybercrime as well. Initially internet was developed as a research tool and information gathering source. With the passage of time internet became more of what transactional in nature with coming up of e- commerce, e- business, e-governance etc. As the world went for digitalization, the area for cybercrime also widened up. In order to deal with this situation there arises a need to have concrete legal structure to combat cybercrime. All legal issues related to internet crime are dealt with through cyber law. While there has been a surge in incidence of cybercrime being committed against women and young girls at large, the Law-making bodies have taken an initiative to protect them against violence and sexual exploitation in the virtual space. The cyber space or say it as a dark world has created haphazard in the society by gradually victimizing the vulnerable female section of our society to fall into hands of cyber-criminals. These agencies have passed certain acts, bills and made amendments in prevailing statues so as to fight this war of cybercrime which is ever increasing.

While construing any legislation due diligence is given to the constitutional provisions. The Indian Constitution provides right to women by virtue of Article 14, 15, 19, 21, 23 and 24, and direct the state to protect the interest of women by framing such policies which contributes towards their social upliftment in the society. It even protects women from any kind of violence to which she is subjected to in cyberspace.

Additionally, the Indian Criminal Justice System lays down certain relevant provisions which protect the women in society against any violent act. The Indian Penal Code, The Code of Criminal Procedure 0f 1973, The Indian Evidence Act are the main postulate of the Indian Criminal Justice System. The Indian Penal Code defines those Acts which are criminal in nature and prescribes punishment for the same. While dealing with crime against women under IPC, section ranging from 354 - 354D and 375 -376E elaborates the sexual offences committed against women to outrage her modesty in the real and virtual world and gives a clear account of penalty inflicted on the person who tend to commit violence against women.

Moreover, there are other various statues enacted to avoid violence committed against women. These statutes especially deal with the women rights and protect them against violence. The IT (Amendment) Act of 2008 inserted some provisions which punished sexual exploitation if the users in cyberspace. But apparently, the Indian legislation has not been able to eliminate cybercrime from the society completely, thus, making it easy for the offender to break laws and commit crime. There are lacunae in our statues as it does not define online crimes against manner in a comprehensive manner, rather they try to include every user in its ambit, and thus making it difficult to ascertain the accountability of the offender.

There might be lacunae in our legal system, but the judiciary has always tried to punish the culprit in a fair manner and deliver justice to the victim. It is the backbone of the democratic setup. The very fact cannot be ignored that judiciary plays a pivotal role in ascertaining the human rights of its citizens and preserving the sanctity of constitution. Judiciary is an independent wing of the government, which interpret the laws in force and resolve dispute between partis and deliver justice to the victim. In order to have a peaceful and well-developed society we require a powerful and transparent adjudicating authority which owes its duty to protect the society from all social evils, and judiciary is the one who protect our rights and promote humanity. The society is ever changing, and at present technology has brought a drastic change in our social setup. It has paved a new way for criminals to commit crime. With the emergence of cybercrime and its repercussion in society and the victim behaviour, poses a challenge for judiciary to prevent the menace of cybercrime. In past few years we have witnessed a gradual surge in the incidence of cyber violence carried out against women in cyber space and the role of judiciary in delivering justice to them. Therefore, the contribution made by judiciary in combatting violence against women in cyberspace is to be appreciated even when the legal statutes fail to provide adequate relief to the victim of crime.

6.2 SUGGESTIONS AND RECOMMENDATIONS

When we speak about offences in a general term, discussion over combating the crime and its negative impact becomes an important aspect. When we talk about any kind of violation to which women and young girls in our society are being subjected to particularly in the virtual space, it ultimately becomes important to have efficient legal and scientific machinery which look into the matter with a great apathy and seeks to avoid any violent against female section of society in up coming future. If we take a step today to eliminate the instances of violation against women today, then we can hope for a better tomorrow for them. It becomes the primary duty of every single individual and a community as a whole to see women as their equal not unequal, and then only we can establish a crime free society for the females in the real and virtual space. After doing a research over victimization of women in cyberspace, it becomes evident to have a discussion over few suggestions which could help in curbing the threat of cyber offences against women.

6.2.1 SENSITISATION OF MASSES

In order to combat the menace of victimization of women in cyberspace, it is important to make people aware about the plight of women in cyberspace. The idea of conducting awareness programmes and campaign is schools, universities, public spaces, government departments, would help the individual to understand how the criminals uses internet and social media platforms to victimize the users and exploit them for monetary gain. Making masses aware about the misuse of internet and the ways they can protect their personal credential from falling into wrong hands would certainly avoid their victimization in cyberspace. Moreover, it becomes important that special awareness programmes about the rights of users and subscribers shall be conducted in urban as well as rural areas, so that in case a victim is not able to complaint about being victimized, then their family members and friends can speak on their behalf.

6.2.2 INCORPORATING CYBERCRIME AND LAWS PERTAINING TO IT INTO ACADEMIC CALENDER

Today, youth are becoming more active users of the internet services and using social media sites the most. They usually spend most of their time on internet and social media sites. Being at a tender age, it gets difficult for them to understand the intention of the criminals and they become soft target for them to victimize. To reduce such incidence, policies should be framed by the education department of introducing a new subject of cybercrimes and laws pertaining to it into academic calendar of schools and colleges, so that the young girls are aware about the harsh reality of the cyber world and how they can avoid their own victimization. By making it a mandatory subject for all students from every field would somehow reduce the number of cybercrimes against young women and girls.

6.2.3 FORMING ONLINE PORTALS TO REDRESS THE GRIEVENCES OF VICTIM:

Due to pressure from society and family members, the victimized women usually avoid complaining about the violence committed against them in cyberspace, and this gives an opportunity to the offender to further exploit her in future. This might worsen up the situation leading to other crime to be committed against women such as abetment to suicide. The best suitable way to eliminate such cases, an online portal shall be made by the law enforcing agency to redress the grievance of cyber attacks on women. This would help the victim to lodge complaint online without any societal pressure, and this would not only help the victim but even the government to collect data on the number of cybercrimes taking place day by day and can work towards framing stringent policies to curb the menace of cybercrime against women.

6.2.4 FRAMING NEW POLICIES WHICH EMPASHISES ON WOMEN PROTECTION IN CYBER SPACE:

Although in India, we have Information Technology Act, 2000 which expressly lays down provisions which define various cybercrime and prescribes punishment for the same, yet it struggles to protect individual interest of women in particular in cyberspace.

The IT Act of 2000 does to expressly defines the cybercrimes committed particularly against women rather it gives an overview about all kind of criminal activities carried through online mode. Therefore, we need a uniform code which is expressly concerned with the cybercrimes committed against women and prescribe harsh punishment to offender.

6.2.5 AMENDING CERTAIN PROVISIONS OF CRIMINAL JUSTICE SYSTEM:

The criminal justice system lays down provisions to punish the offender who commit criminal offence. Though, there are various provisions dealing with crime against women incorporated under Indian Penal Code of 1860, but it does not fully recognize cybercrime committed against women, Certain offences such as online grooming, sextortion and revenge porn still are not recognized as criminal act under the criminal law, thus, making it easy for offender to escape from criminal liability. Therefore, its important that amendment should be made in criminal laws by inserting the abovementioned acts also as an offence against women.

6.2.6 MAKING THE POLICE AND OTHER OFFICIALS ABOUT CYBERCRIMES AND SENSITIZING THEM ABOUT PLIGHT OF WOMEN:

It is the duty of police officer and investigating agencies to initiate a criminal investigation in case a crime is committed. But unfortunately, due to lack of knowledge about technology advancement and the repercussions arising out of its use, make it difficult for them to understand the nature of cybercrime and its impact on women. Due to this reason women usually avoid to lodge complaint about cybercrime committed against them, and this us how various cases go unreported and crime penetrates deep into society. Hence, it becomes important to sensitize the police officials about the cybercrimes and how to deal with its menace.

6.2.7 ESTABLING A COUNSELLING CELL TO GUIDE THE VICTIM AND HER FAMILY

While even today women are expected to remain silent in case they are sexually abused, because it is perceived that if she speaks about her pain, it would bring disrepute to whole family and the society would boycott them. In case, a woman or her relative takes an initiative to complaint about cybercrime incidence, they usually end up taking back their complaint and setting the offender free. To avoid such incidence a special interrogation and counselling cells governed by government shall be established to guide the victim and her family members about her rights and counsel them that it was a mistake committed by victim rather anyone can become a victim of such act so that she is not out under any pressure.

6.2.8 BANNING THE PORN SITES:

This is one of major reason for sexual exploitation of female section of our society in cyberspace. At present there are number of private companies and the service providers who operates the porn sites. There is no strict vigilance to regulate these sites and thus welcoming the offender to abuse women and young girls and make their pornography and publishing the same on these sites to gain monetary benefit. Young and adult secretly enjoy watching the porn movies, and this has resulted in crimes such as rape of women and young girls, sextortion and making revenge porn. Thus, it is important to ban these sites and penalize the offender with harsh punishment.

6.2.9 ESTABLISHING MODERN AND SPECIAL INVESTIGATION CELLS

In order to hasten the speed of fair trial and delivery of justice it is important to have a modern investigating machinery. Investigation has a major role to play when a case is in the court of law. Unlike traditional way of collecting evidence and carry investigation, in cybercrime there is a need for a modern approach and expert guidance to deal with computer related crimes. This can be achieved by establishing a special investigation cell primarily dealing in cybercrime cases.

6.2.10 SETTING UP OF SPECIAL COURTS:

To dispense justice on time it is important to establish special courts consisting of legal experts who are well -versed with the use of Information Technology and cybercrimes. This would administer justice to the victim on time without any delay and punish the offender for violating the laws.

6.2.11 ESTABLISHING EFFIECIENT CYBER SECURITY MACHINERY:

In order to combat the menace of cyber violation against women it becomes necessary to have a cybersecurity machinery which protects the personal information of the users from getting into wrong hands. Like the European Countries where they have special laws relating to cyber security which not only protects the data of users but also regulate the social media sites, to avoid breach of data.

Therefore, the above-mentioned suggestions are based on the observation made while conducting research on the topic -cyber-crime against women. Suggestions mentioned are a cumulative deducted from the loopholes that are there in our legal system and thus, it becomes important to not amend the outdated laws but also create social awareness against cyber-crimes.

6.3 INFERENCE OF DISSERTATION

In summary, the researcher has tried to thoroughly examine the victimization of women in cyberspace and urgent need for special laws which deals particularly in violence committed against women in cyberspace and protect the female section of society from sexual exploitation in the virtual world.

6.3.1 SUMMING -UP OF CHAPTERS OF DISSERTATION

The first chapter of the dissertation gives a brief account of emergence of internet and cybercrime. It explains the reasons for an increase in cybercrime taking place in the virtual world and outlines the concern over victimization of women in particular in cyber space. Further, it elaborates the reason for victimization of women behind the cyber walls and its impact on their personal well -being and on society as whole.

The second chapter of the dissertation gives an insight into the historical advancement of cybercrime and how it has evolved with the passage of time. It elaborates how the traditional crimes have taken over internet and now the conventional crimes are also committed online. It broadly outlines the changing trend of cybercrime from late 80s to present time, and various initiatives taken by worldwide to combat the menace of cybercrime.

The third chapter of the dissertation gives a brief idea about various legislations enacted by the Indian Government to protect the interest of women in cyberspace and promote their welfare in society. It elaborates the rights bestowed under Indian Constitution to safeguard the rights of women and their upliftment in society. Moreover, it defines various sections incorporated under different statues which punishes the perpetrator who commit violence against women in cyberspace. Further, it describes various loopholes present in our legal system while dispensing justice to the victim.

The fourth chapter elaborates the role of judiciary in preserving the rights of female in our society and protecting them against cyber violence.

The fifth chapter gives a brief account of various kinds of cybercrimes committed against women in India in different states and union territories, thus giving a detailed illustration about a surge in number of criminal acts against women.

The sixth chapter simply concludes the dissertation by giving suggestions and recommendation on the bases of research conducted. Further, the suggestions are made by keeping in view the social ser-up of our Indian society and need for a reformative approach in criminal justice system.

6.3.2 ANSWER TO RESEARCH QUESTIONS:

While taking into account the research conducted the researches has tried to answer the questions raised in the dissertation. The first chapter has enlisted the major reasons for the victimization of women in the cyber space. It elaborated various social and personal factors which were the main reason for the frequent violence committed against women in particular. It discusses the patriarchal set up as a major reason for the victimization of women, where women have no say in their personal life also. The plight of women in such that they suffer and cannot complain about their suffering in the patriarchal setup.

The third chapter briefly discuses the various statues enacted to protect the rights of women in cyberspace. Irrespective of having the cyber law, the crime against women in cyberspace is ever increasing. The reason for victimization of women in cyberspace irrespective of having sound provisions to eliminate violence against women is majorly due to the vague provisions in cyber laws and other statues which defines cybercrime as a whole and does not explicitly deals in the women rights. The cyber laws in India enshrined under Information Technology Act, 2000 defines cybercrime in general sense, thus, raising apprehension over the relevance of cyber laws in curbing violence against women. It further describes the liability of the intermediators in preserving the personal data of the users and avoid misuse of their computer resources to commit cyber offence against women.

6.3.3 GIST OF DISSERTATION:

The main postulate of the dissertation is the main reason for victimization of women in cyberspace and the relevant enactments made to combat the threat of violence to which women are subjected in the cyber world. The main reason which has enhanced the crime against women to accelerate is due to easy access to internet services and the suppression of women in our society. Even though we are living in the 21st century where we talk about establishing a community where everyone is treated equally, still gender -biasness prevails in our community. Due to the gender -based crimes which are quite evident in our society, violation against women in cyberspace has gained momentum thus posing threat to the victim survival and challenging the reliability over the outdated legal framework.

After, thoroughly scrutinizing the cases of cyber crimes where women were targeted as mainstream victim. Cyberspace act as a backbone for such criminal acts and provides safe shelter to them. Therefore, it is the need of the hour to have stringent legal provisions which eliminate cybercrime from our society and make the cyber space a better learning platform rather than a mode of committing crime. Every nation state needs to join hands to combat this menace which is not only a threat to users but also to nation security.

7.BIBLIOGRAPHY

7.1 BOOKS

- Narender Kumar, Constitutional Law of India (Allahabad Law Agency, Delhi, 9th Edition, 2015.
- S.N Mishra, Indian Penal Code, (Central Law Publication, 19th Edition, 2015)
- Debarati Halder and K. Jaishankar, Cyber Crimes Against Women in India, Sage Publication, Delhi

7.2 STAUTES

- The Constitution of India
- The Indian Penal Code, 1860
- The Code of Criminal Procedure, 1973
- The Information Technology Act, 2000
- The Protection of Children from Sexual Offences ,2012
- The Immoral Trafficking (Prevention) Act, 1956
- The Indecent Representation of Women (Prohibition) Act, 1986

7.3 JOURNALS

- All India Report
- Supreme Court Cases
- Journal of Human Rights Law and Practice
- National Journal of Cyber Security Law

7.4 ARTICLES

- Ahmed Mateen and Qaiser Abba *"Tsunami of Cybercrime: Analyses of Cyber Crime New Trends, Causes, and remedies In Future prospectus,* "Vol-152, *International Journal of Application*

- Sutapa Saryal, *"Women Right in India: Problem and Prospects"* Vol-3(7)49-53, *International Research Journal of Social Science*

- Mayura U. Pawar, Archana Sakure,*" Cyber space and Women"* Vol -8 , *International Journal of Engineering and Advanced Technology*

7.5 NEWSPAPER

- The Times of India
- The Tribune
- The Hindu
- The Hindustan Times

7.6 WEBLIOGRAPHY

- *https://www.legalserviceindia.com*
- *https://www.blogipleader.in*
- *https://www.lawctopus.in*
- *https://www.hindustantimes.com*
- *https://www.wkipedia.in*
- *https://www.britanica.com*
- *https://www.bbc.com*
- *https://www.ncrb.gov.in*
- *https://www.ssr.com/index.cfm/en/*
- *https://docs.manupatra.in*
- *https://www.vikaspedia.in*
- *https://www.researchgate.net*
- *https://www.ijlmh.com*

www.ingramcontent.com/pod-product-compliance
Lightning Source LLC
Chambersburg PA
CBHW052201220526
45471CB00004B/1770